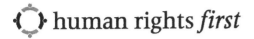

D1621691

Investing in Tragedy

China's Money, Arms, and Politics in Sudan

March 2008

Table of Contents

About Us

Human Rights First believes that building respect for human rights and the rule of law will help ensure the dignity to which every individual is entitled and will stem tyranny, extremism, intolerance, and violence.

Human Rights First protects people at risk: refugees who flee persecution, victims of crimes against humanity or other mass human rights violations, victims of discrimination, those whose rights are eroded in the name of national security, and human rights advocates who are targeted for defending the rights of others. These groups are often the first victims of societal instability and breakdown; their treatment is a harbinger of wider-scale repression. Human Rights First works to prevent violations against these groups and to seek justice and accountability for violations against them.

Human Rights First is practical and effective. We advocate for change at the highest levels of national and international policymaking. We seek justice through the courts. We raise awareness and understanding through the media. We build coalitions among those with divergent views. And we mobilize people to act.

Human Rights First is a non-profit, nonpartisan international human rights organization based in New York and Washington D.C. To maintain our independence, we accept no government funding.

Acknowledgements

Human Rights First would like to extend our warm thanks to the researchers and advisors who contributed to this report, and to the many interns and HRF staff who helped out along the way. We also sincerely thank the Libra Foundation and the Lawson Valentine Foundation for their support of this project.

This report is available for free online at www.humanrightsfirst.org

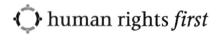 human rights *first*

Headquarters

333 Seventh Avenue
13th Floor
New York, NY 10001-5108

Tel.: 212.845.5200
Fax: 212.845.5299

Washington D.C. Office

100 Maryland Avenue, NE
Suite 500
Washington, DC 20002-5625

Tel: 202.547.5692
Fax: 202.543.5999

www.humanrightsfirst.org

Executive Summary

"China's increasing political and economic stature calls for this country to take on a greater share of responsibility for the health and success of the international system."
—Robert M. Gates, U.S. Defense Secretary

In August, for the first time in history, China will host the Olympics. For Beijing, those will be days of pride, a chance to display its progress and bask in the world's admiration. But far from the splendor of the Summer Games, the people of a remote area in the largest nation in Africa—the people of Sudan's Darfur region—will endure more death, disease and dislocation, and this will be due in no small part to China's callousness. Craving energy to keep its economic miracle humming, Beijing has forged a strong partnership with the Sudanese government in Khartoum.

In the last half-decade, at least 200,000 civilians have died and 2.5 million have been uprooted as Sudan has sought to stamp out a rebellion in Darfur by outfitting local proxy militias to do the job on the ground while Khartoum bombs from above. Their campaign has caused fury around the globe. If China shares such concerns, it hasn't allowed them to break its bond with the Sudanese government, a bond that provides China with oil and markets and provides Khartoum with money, weapons and a shield of legitimacy against international efforts to save the Darfuri people.

As this report illustrates, it is not possible to understand why Darfur's suffering has gone on for so long without understanding how deeply entwined China has become with the Sudanese government, and how this relationship translates into support for Darfur's oppressors. China is Sudan's biggest economic partner, taking 75 percent of its exports. China is Sudan's military mentor, advising its army and giving it guns. It has leverage, a great deal of it. But it has not used that power, preferring to keep cozy with Khartoum to keep the oil flowing. If China had exploited its influence fully, Darfur would be closer to peace and thousands of people might still be alive.

The Lure of Oil

Sudan has vast amounts oil reserves, and has been exporting more and more crude to China. Indeed, nine out of every ten barrels Sudan ships go to China, reaching embarkation ports in pipelines built by Chinese companies and pumped aboard oil tankers at terminals constructed with Chinese help.

Through its state-owned companies, China controls almost all the known oil potential of Sudan. The country has 19 "oil blocks," but only nine are thought to have significant reserves—and China holds the majority rights to drill eight of them at increasing rates.

China's interest in Sudanese oil has no mysterious cause. It will be visible to every Olympic athlete this summer. Each day, Beijing needs another 6.6 million barrels of oil to keep the nation lighted, moving and warm, the greatest thirst in the world after the United States'. Every year, China's economy expands more than ten percent.

Oil has been a prize in the conflicts in Sudan, or at least a key aspect of the background. Most of Sudan's reserves lie in the central or southern parts of the country, and Khartoum has always sought control, both of the oil going out and money coming in. When the large North-South civil war began in 1983, the national government quickly mobilized proxy fighters to evacuate southern villages around two of the newly-discovered oil fields. The proxies did more than that: they burned, looted, and forced children into slavery. Matters only worsened when, in 1989, the Khartoum government was ousted by militants who wanted to impose an even stronger Islamic influence on the nation's political and legal systems.

China has been Khartoum's key partner in developing the infrastructure necessary to extract and transport oil. For instance, it helped develop pipelines that stretch for more than 1,000 kilometers from oil fields to Port Sudan. Chinese state-owed companies helped build Bashair I and II, two huge marine terminals 25 kilometers south of Port Sudan that can hold 400,000 barrels of oil. Sudan owns the terminals, but Chinese companies operate them. China has also invested hundreds of millions of dollars to further develop Sudan's ability to refine the oil it is extracting.

In short, Sudan's oil development has, by and large, been a Chinese production. Beijing's companies pump oil from numerous key fields, which then courses through Chinese-made pipelines to Chinese-made storage tanks to await a voyage to buyers, most of them Chinese. The development of this profitable chain has taken place in close chronological step with the mass atrocities occurring in Darfur. In 2000, before the crisis, Sudan's oil revenue was $1.2 billion. By 2006, with the crisis well underway, that total had shot up 291 percent, to $4.7 billion. How does Sudan use that windfall? Its former finance minister has said that at least 70 percent of the oil profits go to the Sudanese armed forces, linked with its militia allies to the crimes in Darfur.

In the last decade, the Export-Import Bank of China has given Sudan more than $1 billion in "concessional loans," which are low-or-no interest. Traditionally, concessional loans are intended to help poor countries build badly needed projects that are not commercially viable. Sudan, because of its oil revenues, would not seem to need the help that China Export-Import Bank provides. But by giving loans anyway, Beijing buffs its image with Khartoum, ensuring it has access to oil and markets. Beijing looks even more benevolent when it then forgives the loans as it has done on more than one occasion.

Arms for Khartoum

A long tradition of weapons transfers exists between China and Sudan. In the 1960s, China provided at least 18 Mig-17 aircraft to Sudan. In the 1970s, it sold it 130 tanks. In the 1980s, the list included at least 20 aircraft, 50 armored personnel carriers and 50 towed-artillery pieces. Through the long civil wars between North and South in Sudan, China was always on Khartoum's side, militarily.

In the last few years, Khartoum has accelerated its weapons shopping exponentially, using its oil profits, made possible by China. While still seeking heavy weapons—such as tanks and aircraft—it has been aggressively pursuing small arms, precisely the sort a government would need if it wished to equip proxy fighters engaged in Darfur on its behalf. Between 1999 and 2005, a period that includes the start and escalation of the Darfur crisis, Sudan's overall imports of small arms multiplied 680-fold.

Observers in Darfur have reported seeing Chinese weaponry, including grenade launchers and ammunition for assault rifles and heavy machine guns. From 2003 to 2006, China sold over $55 million worth of small arms to Sudan. Since 2004, China has been the near-exclusive provider of small arms to Sudan, supplying on average 90 percent of Khartoum's small arms purchases each year.

A Security Council arms embargo—initially imposed in 2004 under resolution 1556 and expanded in 2005 under resolution 1591—prohibits weapons transfers to Darfur. The government of Sudan, however, has openly stated its refusal to abide by the arms embargo, claiming that it has the sovereign right to transfer weapons into Darfur, which it has continued to do. Faced with the government of Sudan's defiance of its legal obligations, China's continued weapons sales to the government of Sudan, knowing that those weapons have been found in Darfur, puts China in the position of also failing to comply with the embargo.

Just as China bolstered Sudan's ability to refine oil at home, it has bolstered its ability to make weapons at home. Chinese companies assisted in constructing three factories near Khartoum that produce machine guns, rocket launchers, mortars, antitank weapons and ammunition. In addition, Chinese engineers reportedly supervise the work at the Giad industrial complex near Khartoum, which makes even heavier military items, such as tanks and trucks. In the end, most of the ammunition being used in Darfur "is manufactured either in the Sudan or in China," according to a report by the Panel of Experts, which was appointed by the United Nations Security Council to monitor the arms embargo.

China is not merely a prime source of bullets, shells and the means to shoot them. It offers military expertise, too. In October 2005, Chinese commanders and the Sudanese minister of national defense drew up a plan to improve Sudan's armed forces. Even more cooperation was promised in April 2007 at a meeting of the chiefs of each country's armed forces. At that time, Chinese Defense Minister Cao Gangchuan said "military relations between China and Sudan have developed smoothly," and China was ready to do even more.

The North-South civil war drew to a halt in 2005 with the signing of the Comprehensive Peace Agreement (CPA). As part of that deal, oil installations in the South were to be protected jointly by forces from Khartoum and forces from the South, but so far security remains in the hands of Khartoum, either directly or indirectly. The Sudanese

armed forces are deployed near the oil installations, and so are Khartoum-supported "oil police," about 3,000 strong. Further protection for the Chinese oil blocks is provided by militias that are supported by Khartoum. According to a Chinese diplomat, China asked for all this protection in 2004, and there have been unconfirmed reports that China even arms and trains the refinery troops. Whether it does or not, China's assets are being protected.

China's Political Protection

Awakening in 2004 to just how dire the situation in Darfur was becoming, the United Nations Security Council began to think of ways to help. Its first serious response was to discuss what became resolution 1556, which originally threatened Khartoum with economic sanctions if it did not begin to disarm the Janjaweed and prosecute those guilty of atrocities. China put a stop to that effort almost immediately, threatening to veto 1556 unless all language about sanctions was stripped. So they disappeared from the resolution. Even then, China abstained from voting on the remnants of the original, as if even the revised resolution would be too much for its friends in Khartoum.

Later that same year, as violence continued in Darfur, the United Nations (U.N.) tried again. Once again, there was a call for punitive steps. Once again, China blocked them. Once again, it abstained from the vote on the gutted result. Once again, it said that sanctions just make a bad situation worse. A few days later, Sudanese President Bashir praised Beijing, along with the three other countries that had abstained, Algeria, Pakistan and Russia. They were Sudan's "true friends," Bashir said.

At almost every turn, international efforts to protest and end the suffering in Darfur have collided with China's willingness to stand up for Khartoum. China has consistently deflected pressure, emboldened its obstructionism and, of course, protected the two nations' myriad deals and connections. Between 2004 and October 2007, the Security Council debated 14 substantive resolutions about Darfur, and China has used its power to weaken nine of them, forcing the removal of tough language, including economic sanctions.

On March 31, 2005, the Security Council did manage to refer the Darfur crisis to the prosecutor for the International Criminal Court for consideration of possible war crimes. China did not use its veto to block the referral. Indeed, after 20 months of investigation, the prosecutor found enough evidence to issue arrest warrants for two people, charging them with crimes committed in 2003 and 2004. One was Ali Mohamed Ali Abdel Rahman, a leader of the Janjaweed. The other was Ahmad Haroun, the Sudanese minister of humanitarian affairs.

In response to the arrest warrants, Khartoum called the prosecutor a "junior employee doing cheap work." It said there have been no war crimes in Darfur, and, in effect, that even if there have been, only the Sudanese courts have the competence to deal with them. So the two men were free to move about the country. After the indictments were issued, Haroun was given a new responsibility: he became the official in charge of relief work in the refugee camps.

A Shifting Policy?

In May 2006, Khartoum and a rebel faction signed the Darfur Peace Agreement, which led to discussions at the U.N. about deploying 26,000 foreign troops to separate the rebels and Khartoum-backed militias. Initially, Khartoum greeted the idea of a peacekeeping force with Cold War rhetoric, denouncing it as a form of neo-imperialism. China fought at the Security Council to strip the U.N. troops of the one tool they would need to keep the peace: the power to use force when necessary. China lost that fight, but Sudan thanked it for the effort. "We do appreciate the support that China has given us in the Security Council," President Bashir said on a visit to Beijing shortly after passage of the peacekeeping resolution.

Under international pressure, China began slowly to revise its position and urged Khartoum to acquiesce to

the force, though it did so privately. It pledged to assign 275 Chinese military engineers to help with the force deployment. It offered $10 million in humanitarian relief. It named a special envoy for Darfur, who even said he had told Khartoum that China was concerned that its weapons were, in fact, winding up on the Darfuri battlefield.

Eventually, Khartoum agreed to the peacekeeping force. China heralded the decision as proof of the wisdom of its close relationship with Sudan. It had used its influence for a good cause, and wanted credit.

But as China pushed Khartoum on the peacekeeping force last year, it signed a $1.2 billion deal to build rail links between Khartoum and Port Sudan, forgave $80 million in Sudanese debt and turned over a $12.9 million loan for the presidential palace. Last year, as Bashir balked at a peacekeeping force and the U.N. once again spoke of sanctions, China smothered that discussion, just as it had earlier ones about sanctions. All those steps hardly reflect a China pressuring its ally.

So far, China has not paid much of a price for remaining close to Sudan, and the oil continues to flow to the Chinese economy. But there is a real risk for China. To keep its economic miracle going, and to keep at bay democratic urges among its own people, China needs what any capitalist state needs: stability in markets and a guarantee that its investments are safe. But by consistently siding with a rogue regime in Khartoum, China puts this stability at risk. The government in Khartoum might not always be there to protect China's investments and needs, and how would the next leaders feel about China's heavy-handed role? Memories are long. The oil might not always flow.

"China is enemy number one," said an official of the southern side in the North-South civil war. "They are the ones who kept Bashir in power for so long, providing him with weapons to try and win the war in the South. They are the ones who supplied him with helicopter gun ships on the attacks on Bentiu and other places. They are evil. They are the ones providing military support to the government on Darfur. Of course they are."

In fact, the future might already be happening. Under the terms of the 2005 agreement to end the North-South civil war, the new Government of Southern Sudan (GOSS) has the right to hold a referendum in 2011 on whether to secede. If it did secede, it would likely take with it many of Sudan's oil fields. The South has complained for years that it does not get a fair share of revenue from those fields, and has made it clear that whatever deals were negotiated between Khartoum and China about drilling rights and pipelines may no longer hold.

If the specter of South Sudan's separation makes China nervous, it is a less immediate threat than the activism inspired by the Olympics. China continues to claim that it has limited influence with Khartoum. Besides, the Special Representative of the Chinese Government on the Darfur Issue, Liu Guijin, said China has already used its influence by urging Sudan to accept a peacekeeping force. Despite these protestations, China is clearly feeling the heat. The Chinese special envoy's recent five-day visit to Sudan is evidence of that. The Olympics are at risk of looking less like the grand ratification of Chinese success, and more like a reminder of what China has not done for Darfur.

The Chinese public relations campaign to simultaneously belittle the extent of its influence in Sudan and claim credit for playing a positive role has kicked into high gear. But if Beijing wants admiration at the Olympics, it must do more, far more, to stop the atrocities that continue in Darfur and ensure that those most responsible for these crimes are brought to justice. In the final chapter of this report, Human Rights First makes several recommendations for concrete actions China can take to demonstrate its commitment to peace, justice and stability in Sudan. First and foremost, China should:

- Immediately terminate arms transfers to all parties involved in the conflict in Darfur, including the Sudanese government, to ensure that the embargo imposed by Security Council resolutions 1556 (2004) and 1591 (2005) is fully implemented. China also should immediately terminate any other form of military support to the Sudanese government, including training activities.

- Support the expansion of the U.N. Security Council arms embargo on Darfur to the whole of Sudan and prohibit the sale and supply of arms and related materiel to non-state armed groups located in or operating from Chad.

- Use its influence to guarantee that the African Union/United Nations peacekeeping operation authorized by the Security Council (UNAMID) be deployed to Darfur immediately. China should urge the government of Sudan to accept unconditionally the composition of the operation proposed by the United Nations and to remove all legal, administrative, and practical impediments to troop deployment. Should Sudan continue to evade its legal obligations by obstructing the full and immediate deployment of UNAMID, China should support efforts in the U.N. Security Council to place targeted sanctions on key Sudanese government officials, including President Omar al-Bashir. Additionally, China also should help fund and commit additional troops for the UNAMID operation and help supply the 24 transport and security helicopters needed by UNAMID to help ensure that the mission can operate effectively.

- Publicly support efforts to hold individuals in Sudan accountable for committing mass atrocities at the International Criminal Court (ICC). Specifically, China should urge Sudan to immediately comply with the warrants issued by the ICC for the arrest of Ahmad Harun and Ali Kushayb and to surrender to the ICC these two individuals who face multiple charges of crimes against humanity and war crimes in Darfur. Should Sudan continue to evade its legal obligation to comply with the ICC arrest warrants, China should support efforts in the United Nations Security Council to place targeted sanctions on key Sudanese government officials, including President Omar al-Bashir.

Money

"The Chinese are very nice ... They don't have anything to do with any politics or problems."
—Awad Ahmed al Jaz, Sudanese Minister for Energy

The rapid growth of China's economy over the last three decades has forced China to seek energy resources outside its borders. Through trade and international investment, Chinese per capita gross domestic product (GDP) has increased more than thirteen-fold since 1970, and, on average, the country's economy grew more than eight percent annually between 2000 and 2005.[1]

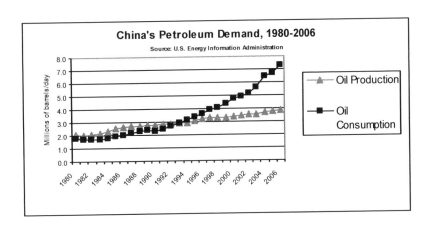

China's Quest for Energy

With this sustained economic development and the resulting increased standards of living, demand for energy in China has skyrocketed. Between 2000 and 2005, for example, China's consumption of electricity rose more than 83 percent, and its overall energy consumption rose more than 78 percent.[2] Car ownership in China has increased over ten percent annually,[3] and by 2030 there will be approximately 390 million cars on China's roads, more than 20 times the number in 2002.[4]

China's domestic oil and gas resources are inadequate to meet the country's needs, resulting in massive oil imports. In 2006, China consumed nearly 7.6 million barrels of oil each day, of which nearly 47 percent was imported.[5] Today, China is the world's second largest consumer of oil, and the third largest oil importing country.[6] China will need to import an estimated 60 percent of the oil it will consume by the year 2020.[7] For the indefinite future, then, China's economic growth depends on significantly increasing oil imports.

China has been willing to fill these needs by buying oil and other resources from countries that are being pressured or even shunned by other nations. These governments welcome a strong relationship with China, unfettered by the demands for good governance or adherence to human rights standards required by other international lenders. By giving these governments the funding they would otherwise obtain with difficulty, if at all, China weakens the ability of the broader international community to promote human rights in these countries. As Sudanese Minister of Energy Awad Ahmed al Jaz explained, "The Chinese are very nice ... They don't have anything to do with any politics or problems."[8]

China's vast influence with the government of Sudan stems from its economic and military investments in that country combined with the political patronage it wields to shield the Sudanese government from censure. The depth and breadth of its investments and their impact on Khartoum's ability not only to formulate but also to carry out a domestic policy in Darfur that violates international human rights law, contradict China's claims that it does not interfere in Sudan's sovereign affairs. In fact, China's ongoing support for Khartoum enables the Sudanese government to continue to pursue its violations of international law.

China's "Non-Interference" Policy: Rhetoric or Reality?

China explains its unconditional partnerships through the lens of a policy of "non-interference in the internal affairs of other sovereign states." Following China's "100 Years of Humiliation"—the legacy of the Japanese invasion and a violent civil war between the Kuomintang and Communist parties—China very cautiously opened the country's economy to development in the 20th century. Non-interference enabled China to slowly leave its self-imposed isolation behind. Non-interference has also served as a bulwark against international criticism of China for its treatment of Tibet and its view of Taiwan as a "renegade province."

Thwarting Taiwan's efforts at independence has become a top priority in China's foreign policy. In searching for allies on the Taiwan question, China has looked to African countries for support.[9] It has not been disappointed; in September 2007, when the United Nations General Assembly decided for the fifteenth year not to address Taiwan's bid for U.N. membership, China thanked African countries for blocking Taiwan's membership.[10] As this report will show, China has rewarded that loyalty in kind to Sudan with political protection on one of Khartoum's policy priorities, Darfur.

Against the background of its non-interference and Taiwan policies, China's expanding energy needs have become a key factor shaping the government's foreign policy objectives. In pursuit of these needs, state-controlled oil companies have undertaken aggressive campaigns to expand oil extraction around the globe, regardless of the human rights records of resource-rich trading partners.

China's search for foreign oil revealed that many markets were already dominated by western companies. Consequently, China turned to countries such as Iran, Iraq, Sudan, and Burma, where concerns about gross human rights abuses or security issues limited western investment but did not constrain China. Hamed Elneel Abdel Gadeir, Sudan's deputy secretary general of the Ministry of Energy and Mining, stated that "It was not our choice to look East, but when we looked West, all the doors were closed."[11] Sudanese President Omar al-Bashir welcomed his country's growing relations with China, saying that when western oil companies withdrew from Sudan, "that allowed us to turn to the East ... And the East has never let us down."[12]

The Problem with Non-interference

"[A]ll the people of Darfur believe that China is a partner for this genocidal government in Khartoum."

> —Spokesperson for the Justice and Equality Movement, on the group's kidnapping of five workers in an October 2007 attack on Chinese oil operations.

China's close economic ties to repressive states both obstruct international efforts to promote human rights, and also carry hazardous political consequences for China. Some of China's partner governments—Sudan, Burma, and Zimbabwe—are widely known to pursue policies of mass human rights abuses. China refuses to condemn the perpetrating regimes for these mass abuses while it supports them financially, militarily, and politically.

Both the massive investment by Chinese state-owned companies and the government's unconditional international aid shapes the politics along with the economies in these countries. Officials within the Chinese foreign ministry acknowledge privately that economic involvement does constitute "interference," and that this recognition has moved some to reassess the principle of non-interference.[13]

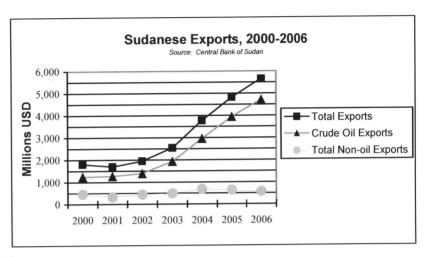

Sudanese Exports, 2000-2006
Source: Central Bank of Sudan

Recent events have begun to indicate that Beijing's support for rights-abusing regimes may undermine the billions of dollars it has invested overseas. As more Chinese laborers travel abroad to work for Chinese companies in Sudan, for example, they find themselves at heightened risk of attack by local populations outraged by China's support for an abusive host government.[14]

This connection was made explicitly by the Darfur rebel group that recently took five hostages in an attack on Chinese oil operations in the Kordofan region. The group gave the Chinese-led consortium, the Greater Nile Petroleum Operating Company (GNPOC), one week to leave Sudan, asserting, "[a]ll the people of Darfur believe that China is a partner for this genocidal government in Khartoum."[15] In Ethiopia, members of the Ogaden National Liberation Front independence group killed nine Chinese workers and kidnapped seven after warning that investment in the Ogaden region that benefited the Ethiopian government "would not be tolerated."[16] In Zambia, a presidential candidate ran on an anti-China platform, suggesting that he would recognize Taiwan's independence if elected because China has undercut

local industries, created hazardous working conditions, and offered low wages at Chinese-run copper mines.[17] These incidents illustrate the statement of Elijah Aleng, deputy governor of the Sudanese Central Bank, who said "[W]hen you exploit oil and resources and nothing goes to the population, then you are financing the war against them with resources and that is negative."[18]

China's non-interference policy not only puts Chinese nationals working on the ground at risk, it also imperils China's economic growth strategy as a whole. By supporting rights-abusing regimes, China may find itself out of favor in case of a change in government. For example, if oil-rich Southern Sudan does secede from Sudan, China may find itself in trouble with this newly-formed country, many of whose citizens believe Beijing has propped up Khartoum's rule for decades.[19] The damage to Chinese investments might be like that to U.S. oil projects in Iran thirty years ago.

Oil Beckons

Through its state-owned companies, China controls almost all the known oil potential of Sudan. The country has 19 "oil blocks," but only nine are thought to have significant reserves—and China holds the majority rights to drill eight of them. China's quest for oil is a necessary, if not sufficient, element in Beijing's continued growth— which includes construction for the Olympics.

China has continued to expand its presence in Sudan's oil sector despite the government of Sudan's perpetration of—or at least support for—mass human rights violations. In the past two years, the China National Petroleum Corporation (CNPC), which is entirely state-owned, has been awarded majority stakes in two oil blocks—35 percent of Block 15 in 2005 and 40 percent of Block 13 in 2007. [20] Negotiations leading to these two deals took place as violence raged in Darfur and as the international spotlight shone on Khartoum's massive abuses.

Oil and War: A Volatile Mix

Although Chevron discovered Sudan's oil in the 1970s, development of the industry was delayed in part due to the North-South civil war. Tensions between North and South Sudan stem from religious, cultural, and linguistic differences. Since before independence from Britain in 1955, there have been wars rooted in these regional divisions, the most recent erupting in 1983 when the central government—controlled by northerners—imposed strict Islamic law on the entire country and declared Arabic the official language. The Sudan People's Liberation Army (SPLA) took up arms in quest of greater autonomy and power for the pre-dominantly Christian and Animist South.

In 1999, a new factor was introduced into the war: oil extraction and its resulting wealth. It was not until that year that the country became a net oil exporter. Sudan's oil revenues then grew at a sharp pace, increasing more than eight-fold in just a few years, from an estimated $61 million in 1999 to an estimated $596 million in 2001. [21] Much of the hard currency pouring into Khartoum's coffers was spent on armaments. Sudan's former finance minister and former transportation minister put defense spending at over 70 to 80 percent of the government's revenue from oil. [22] Given that China is the primary purchaser of Sudanese oil, China appears to be the chief funder of Khartoum's weapons acquisitions.

After 21 years of conflict, the Comprehensive Peace Agreement (CPA) brought a tenuous peace to the South in 2005. By this time, more than two million Sudanese had lost their lives from violence, disease, or starvation as a result of the North-South war. An additional four million were made homeless, and 600,000 were forced to flee the country as refugees. [23] Signed by Khartoum and the SPLA (subsequently recast as a political party known as the Southern People's Liberation Movement/Army, or SPLM/A), the CPA provides that Khartoum and the Government of Southern Sudan (GOSS) will equally share revenues from oil extraction. [24]

An Uncertain Future for Oil Contracts

China's dominance in Sudan's oil sector relies on its many contracts with Khartoum. But the threat of renewed conflict in South Sudan, as well as of secession by the South, puts these contracts at great risk. The CPA mandates that contracts signed before the CPA's resolution will remain binding and envisions the creation of a National Petroleum Commission—comprising the president of Sudan, the GOSS president, four members of each of the two governments, and three members from the province producing the oil—to negotiate and approve future oil contracts. [25]

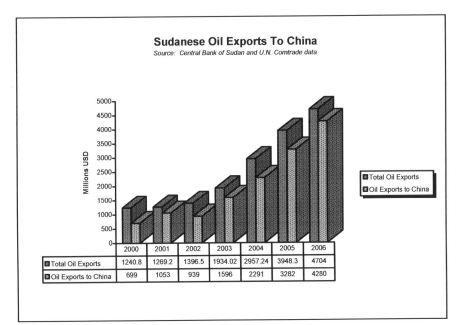

Sudanese Oil Exports To China
Source: Central Bank of Sudan and U.N. Comtrade data

	2000	2001	2002	2003	2004	2005	2006
Total Oil Exports	1240.8	1269.2	1396.5	1934.02	2957.24	3948.3	4704
Oil Exports to China	699	1053	939	1596	2291	3282	4280

the North-South war—marginalization and lack of development—underlie the violence in Darfur, which threatens to undermine the CPA at the same time that it has been a tragedy for millions in western Sudan.

Even if these conflicts originally stemmed from marginalization and a crisis of governance, oil wealth now plays a key role, at least in the calculations of the various parties. Revenues from Sudan's crude oil exports nearly quadrupled in six years, from approximately $1.2 billion in 2000[28] to more than $4.7 billion in 2006 (a figure larger than the entire gross national products of more than forty countries).[29] At the same time, oil exports grew from 69 percent to more than 83 percent of the country's total exports.[30] During the same period exports overall grew significantly, but the growth came almost entirely from increased crude oil exports as non-oil exports remained almost flat.[31]

China's Dominance in Sudan's Economy

"[If] they bring the money we will give them more oil ... the sky's the limit."

> —Awad Ahmed al-Jaz, Sudanese Minister of Energy and Mining, on the future of Sudanese oil sales to China

China is Sudan's largest trading partner overall, serving as the destination for more than three-quarters of Sudan's exports in 2006.[32] Oil accounts for a large percentage of Sudan's exports to China and, as Beijing focuses on developing long-term sources of energy, Sudan's importance to China could increase. Sudan

The CPA also mandates that nationwide elections be held in 2009 following a census, and that Southern Sudan will hold a referendum in 2011 to decide whether to remain a part of Sudan or to secede and become independent. [26] It is highly possible that the nationwide presidential elections will be delayed, as the prerequisite census has yet to be undertaken.

Perhaps as a result of Khartoum's apparent bad faith in implementing many of the CPA's provisions, including the equitable division of oil revenues, sources within Southern Sudan's government have indicated that if the region votes to secede in 2011, it will renegotiate—rather than continue without modification—all oil contracts involving fields within Southern Sudan.[27] Investors are unlikely to welcome this lack of predictability regarding a substantial portion of Sudan's total oil reserves. Even more troubling for investors is the fact that many of Sudan's most productive fields straddle the North-South border, the inevitable front line in any renewed armed conflict.

The CPA, despite its imperfections, has at least temporarily halted combat between the Khartoum government and the SPLM/A. But many of the same complaints that drove seems a willing partner, sending more than 92 percent of its petroleum and petroleum products to China in the first quarter of 2007.[33] The volume of oil exported from Sudan to China over the first half of 2007 has seen a five-fold increase.[34] The Sudanese government apparently sees no limits to this trade: as the Sudanese Minister of Energy and Mining, Awad Ahmed al-Jaz, said of the Chinese in 2006, "[If] they bring the money we will give them more oil ... the sky's the limit."[35]

Although the relationship between China and Sudan is rooted in the oil industry, Chinese companies are active in other sectors of Sudan's economy as well, most notably in infrastructure development. These projects are quite lucrative to the Chinese companies involved, but because those companies are state-owned and the projects are largely financed by Chinese credit, this commercial activity also has political consequences: solidifying ties between the two governments.

In most instances, Chinese state-owned companies have acquired direct ownership interests in Sudan's crude oil, allowing China to bypass international oil markets and negotiate resource pricing directly with the Khartoum government.[36] These companies oversee every step in the process of bringing Sudanese crude oil to Chinese refineries. They receive instructions from the Beijing government and are motivated not only by purely commercial ends but by Chinese state interests as well.

The China National Petroleum Corporation: A Driving Force in Sudan

The most important Chinese oil company operating in Sudan is the China National Petroleum Corporation (CNPC), a wholly state-owned entity that is China's largest supplier of crude oil and natural gas.[37] CNPC is a giant in the global arena; ranked twenty-fourth on the 2007 Fortune Global 500 list, the company had 2007 revenues of more than $110 billion.[38]

The relationship between CNPC and Sudan is symbiotic: not only is CNPC the largest foreign investor in the Sudanese oil sector, but Sudan is CNPC's largest market for overseas investment.[39] Through its equity ownership in

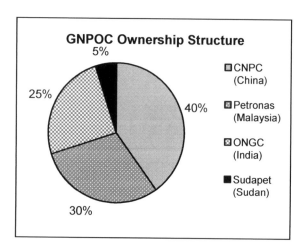

GNPOC Ownership Structure

- CNPC (China) — 40%
- Petronas (Malaysia) — 30%
- ONGC (India) — 25%
- Sudapet (Sudan) — 5%

various oil extraction consortia, CNPC controls hundreds of thousands of barrels per day of oil in Sudan, all of which is exported to China. This partnership is mutually beneficial: China helped Sudan develop its oil industry at a time when others would not, and Sudan provided China with an oil market that other countries shunned and an entry into the African oil market as a whole.[40]

CNPC was initially able to gain a foothold after Canadian companies—first Talisman, then Arakis—had to withdraw from Sudan due to legal, shareholder, and U.S. government pressure.[41] It rapidly expanded its interests. CNPC signed its first contracts for operations in Sudan's Block 6 in 1995,[42] while Sudanese President Bashir was visiting China.[43] By 1997, CNPC was able to buy in as the largest stakeholder in a Sudanese oil development consortium, the Greater Nile Petroleum Operating Company (GNPOC). The above graph illustrates the ownership of GNPOC.

Today, GNPOC comprises four oil companies, and CNPC is the operator for the consortium's extraction projects in Sudan. GNPOC holds the development rights to the country's most lucrative oil fields, Blocks 1, 2, and 4 in the Muglad Basin,[44] with estimated recoverable reserves of between 600 million and 1.2 billion barrels of petroleum.[45] This may prove to be nearly one-quarter of all oil in Sudan. Put into production in 1999, these blocks were the only source of Sudanese oil production until 2005. CNPC, as the largest stakeholder in GNPOC and operator of Blocks 1, 2, and 4, is believed to have invested more than $4 billion dollars in the development of these fields.[46] During 2005-2006, GNPOC drilled at least 10 new wells in Blocks 1, 2 and 4.[47] One of these, Neem 3, is believed to hold the highest individual well production in the Muglad Basin. In July 2006, production began in the Neem oilfield at 24,000 barrels per day, but GNPOC plans to ultimately increase that production to 40,000 barrels per day.[48]

CNPC, either directly or through its interest in various consortia, also owns the rights to develop Blocks 3, 6, 7, 13, and 15.[49] CNPC is the largest stakeholder (with a 41 percent interest) in Petrodar, a consortium that owns the rights to develop Sudan's Blocks 3 and 7 in the Melut Basin. Petrodar's first export of oil took place in August 2006.[50] Production from fields located in these blocks totaled approximately 165,000 barrels per day as of January 2007,[51] with Petrodar planning to increase production to 250,000 barrels per day by the end of 2007 and 300,000 per day in 2008.[52] The fields located in these blocks have estimated recoverable reserves of more than 460 million barrels.[53] If production in fact continues at the projected 300,000 barrels per day beyond 2008, those reserves will be exhausted in just over three years. Petrodar's total cost in developing Blocks 3 and 7 to production is estimated to have been $1.4 billion.[54]

CNPC also directly owns 95 percent of the rights to develop Block 6, an area adjacent to the land under development by GNPOC.[55] This block is currently producing approximately 40,000 barrels per day, with the capacity to produce twice that amount.[56] In March 2007, CNPC put a new pipeline into service linking Block 6 to the main pipeline transporting oil to Port Sudan.[57]

Sudan's Oil Infrastructure: A Chinese Production

The governments of China and Sudan have taken their oil-based relationship beyond extraction. Sudan's most productive oil fields are located deep within the country's interior, requiring the construction of a system of pipelines and pumping stations to transport oil from its fields to the export terminal at Port Sudan.

Pipelines

Sudan's oil pipelines were entirely constructed by Chinese companies. The longest of them covers more than 1,500 kilometers from Block 1, in Unity State, to Port Sudan, picking up oil from Blocks 2 and 4 on the way. The pipeline is operated by GNPOC and was constructed by CNPC through its wholly-owned engineering subsidiary China Petroleum Engineering Construction Corporation (CPECC).[58] CPECC brought an estimated 10,000 Chinese workers to Sudan in 1999 to complete the project in advance of the ten-year anniversary of the seizure of power by Bashir.[59]

The vice president of CPECC reportedly boasted of the speed with which this difficult project was completed saying that "A Western company couldn't have done what we did ... Sudan wanted it done in 18 months and we did it."[60] It was rumored that CPECC had kept their bid for the project low by planning to bring prisoners from China to work on the pipeline. While it is not clear whether this plan came to fruition, the Chinese work force on the project certainly endured harsh conditions, working in the searing heat for up to 14 hours each day.[61]

Sudan's other major pipeline runs 1,000 kilometers from Blocks 3/7, which are operated by Petrodar, to Port Sudan. It was built by engineering subsidiaries of the China Petrochemical Corporation, also known as Sinopec Group, which is China's largest company by revenue, ranking seventeenth worldwide in the most recent Fortune Global 500. It is also China's second-largest oil company, behind CNPC.[62] Sinopec Group is entirely state-owned, although shares in some of its subsidiaries are publicly traded. Sinopec Group's oil extraction rights in Sudan are much more limited than those of CNPC, holding only six percent of the Petrodar consortium, which holds the development rights for Blocks 3 and 7.

However, through two Sinopec subsidiaries—Sinopec International Petroleum Service Corp (SIPSC) and Zhongyuan Petroleum Exploration Bureau International

Corporation (ZPEB)—Sinopec has completed numerous engineering projects in Sudan, including the Block 3/7 pipeline. SIPSC received the contract and ZPEB served as a subcontractor on this project, building nearly 500 kilometers of the pipeline.[63] SIPSC awarded another subcontract to CPECC. According to one ZPEB official, the overall cost of the pipeline was expected to exceed $100 million.[64]

These oilfield services and construction projects support the government of China in achieving three goals: to garner revenue through lucrative construction contracts, to distinguish itself from its competitors, and to build the elements necessary to ensure and expand China's long-term supply of energy from Sudan. The speed at which Chinese companies build in Sudan is costly. CPECC claimed that it failed to make a profit in its construction of several projects: the al Jeili refinery, an enormous oil field surface engineering project, and the Block 1/2/4 pipeline.[65] Although some observers have questioned the accuracy of these assertions, it is plausible that the Chinese state-owned contractors were willing to carry out these massive projects without direct financial gain in order to speed up the process of extracting oil from Sudan—destined for its own market—and to promote its relationship with Sudan.

Other Oil-Related Infrastructure

Chinese companies' infrastructure work extends beyond the water's edge in Port Sudan. Subsidiaries of CNPC and Sinopec Group were involved in the development of two marine terminals (Bashair I and II) for the loading and storage of more than 400,000 barrels of oil destined for export.[66] These terminals are located approximately 25 kilometers south of Port Sudan. Although the Sudanese government owns both terminals, GNPOC is the operator for Terminal I[67] and Petrodar operates Terminal II, inaugurated only in July 2007.[68] CNPC subsidiary CPECC has been the primary subcontractor for the construction and development of both terminals;[69] and the 2004 contract to build Beshair II, and part of the pipeline from blocks 3/7 to the terminal, was worth $405 million to CPECC.[70]

China has been a key partner in developing Sudan's refining industry. Despite its oil reserves, Sudan had been importing refined petroleum because it did not have enough refining capability at home. CNPC has been involved from the start at al Jeili, Sudan's main refinery and one of only two refineries in Sudan that allow the country to refine its own crude oil for domestic consumption.[71] Al Jeili was jointly built by CNPC (through CPECC) and Khartoum, with each owning 50 percent of the operating company.[72] It began operating in 2000, although it quickly became insufficient for Sudan's growing refining needs.[73] When Sudan decided to upgrade the refinery, CNPC paid its share (nearly $300 million),[74] and the Chinese government loaned Sudan more than $60 million toward its portion of the upgrade costs. The loan was collateralized by Sudanese crude oil, which is also the means of repayment to China.[75]

Human Rights Consequences of China's Oil Development in Sudan

Between extraction, transportation, storage, refining, and even use of oil, the development of Sudan's oil industry has been a Chinese production. It has allowed Chinese companies to quickly extract and transport crude oil for export at the same time that it has enabled the Bashir regime to consolidate its hold on power by generating more funds to carry out its policies by the elite inner circle. Given that oil is Sudan's major export and therefore creates myriad jobs, power bases, and wealth, these close economic links have far-reaching effects, both economic and political, throughout Sudan. In addition, in the first year after the completion of the GNPOC pipeline and the Al Jeili refinery, Sudan's finance and energy ministers estimated that the country would save between $300 million and $500 million annually by eliminating its costly oil imports.[76]

The profitability of Sudan's oil sector has developed in close chronological step with the violence in Darfur. In 2000, before the crisis, Sudan's oil revenue was $1.2 billion. By 2006, with the crisis well underway, that total had shot up 291 percent, to $4.7 billion. How does

Sudan use that windfall? Its finance minister has said that at least 70 percent of the oil profits go to the Sudanese armed forces, linked with its militia allies to the crimes in Darfur.

Oil exploitation has also coincided with a decline in the rural population in provinces surrounding the oil fields. In parts of Melut and Maban provinces, more than 15,000 civilians, primarily local Dinka and Maban populations, have been forcibly displaced.[77] This displacement appears to be part of a pattern in which Sudan's security forces engage in human rights abuses to further the country's oil development.

Beyond Oil: Other Infrastructure Projects in Sudan

China's role in Sudan is not limited to the oil industry. Chinese companies are involved with several other projects which, though they aim to improve the country's badly neglected infrastructure, have been highly controversial. The biggest of these are two massive hydroelectric dams and railway line from Khartoum to Port Sudan.

The Khartoum-Port Sudan Railway

In early 2007, while stalling the international community's efforts to help bring peace to Darfur, the government of Sudan signed an agreement with the China Railway Engineering Group, a state-owned entity, for the development of the rail lines between Khartoum and Port Sudan. This deal has been valued at $1.15 billion, making it the largest capital investment agreement to date between the two countries.[78] With this deal, China bolstered Khartoum at a time when much of the rest of the international community was trying to send the opposite signal.

Merowe Dam

The Merowe Dam, the largest hydroelectric project in all of Africa since the construction of the Aswan High Dam in Egypt in the 1960s,[79] is expected to double Sudan's electricity generation capability.[80] Although the project had been contemplated since the early years of the 20th century, it was not revisited in earnest until Sudan's economy recently boomed thanks to oil.

When complete, the Merowe Dam will have cost over $1.9 billion.[81] Despite this enormous price tag, the Chinese-led consortium leading the construction reportedly undercut competing bidders by more than ten percent.[82] More than 20 percent of the overall cost,[83] nearly $400 million,[84] was financed through Chinese government loans provided by the Export-Import Bank of China. The Chinese Consortium for the Merowe Dam (CCMD) is made up of two Chinese companies, the China International Water and Electric Corporation (CWE) and the China National Water Resources and Hydropower Engineering Corporation (CWHEC, or Sinohydro), both of which are state-owned.[85] Other firms involved in the project include Alstom (France), Lahmeyer International (Germany), and ABB (Switzerland). In addition, a CNPC subsidiary won a subcontract for the Merowe Dam project; this is the subsidiary's first large overseas project and it has expressed hope that it will gain valuable international experience in connection with the project.[86]

Like many large dams, Merowe has had destructive human and environmental impacts. The dam will create a reservoir running approximately 200 kilometers, resulting in the forced displacements of approximately 50,000 civilians.[87] More than 10,000 civilians already have been resettled against their will on land so poor that even with irrigation, farmers cannot produce subsistence crops, much less grow food to sell. When citizens have met to organize opposition to the dam, armed militia groups have opened fire on them.[88] The environmental impact is no less deleterious: independent evaluation of the impact assessment for the dam project revealed that the builders ignored the likelihood of damage to water quality, aquatic life, and public health.[89]

Kajbar Dam

Chinese companies have been just as involved with the similarly problematic Kajbar Dam, and have provided $200 million to date toward its construction, in addition to expertise for technical studies.[90] The dam is expected to produce 300 megawatts of electricity.[91] Kajbar Dam, located along the Nile River near the Egypt-Sudan border is a joint project by the Sudanese Kajbar Hydroelectric Company and two Chinese firms, the International Water and Electricity Company and the Machinery Export and Import Company, both of which are state-owned. Through these two companies, the Chinese government committed to covering at least 85 percent of the investment of the facility, as much as $400 million[92] with the Sudanese government responsible for the remainder.[93]

The Kajbar Dam and an associated reservoir will submerge 30 villages,[94] home to approximately 60,000 people,[95] the country's last remaining concentration of Nubian tribes, and important Nubian archaeological sites.[96] Sudan's Nubian population, uniting to resist the dam,[97] managed to shut the project down for seven years.[98] The government of Sudan responded to these protests by sending in riot police and security units to break up demonstrations.[99] In June 2007, police shot dead four protestors who were attacking construction equipment,[100] and arrested demonstrators as well as journalists traveling to the region to investigate the demonstrations and reports of violence.[101] Observers fear that the situation could deteriorate further, potentially resulting in armed conflict.[102] In addition to this potentially worsening civil unrest,[103] environmental groups have also expressed concern over the negative impacts on the Nile River ecosystem.

China holds up the Merowe and Kajbar dams as examples of positive economic development.[104] But by investing in these dams, China is not only enabling human rights violations in Sudan, but is losing money (in the case of Kajbar) in the process; the only clear winner here is the government of Sudan.

Funding the Construction: Concessional Loans serving China's Foreign Policy

Thanks to the oil infrastructure, the railway, and the dams, Sudan owes Chinese companies a great deal of money. In the last decade, the Export-Import Bank of China (China Exim Bank),[105] the government-run export credit agency, has given Sudan more than $1 billion in "concessional loans," which are low or no-interest. China Exim Bank gave $200 million for Kajbar Dam, $300 million for Merowe Dam, $349 million for two power stations, $3.6 million for a conference hall. And it gave $12.9 million for a new presidential palace.

China Exim Bank, while nominally independent, seeks to advance the government's policies through the use of economic tools, often in concert with political and military efforts. Perhaps most important for Beijing's foreign policy is the role of China Exim Bank in administering concessional loans to developing countries, including Sudan. These loans feature favorable lending and repayment terms for projects that assist in local development and might not otherwise obtain commercial financing.[106] China's concessional loans to Sudan have strengthened both its relationship with Khartoum and its access to Sudan's energy resources.

The China Exim Bank focuses on projects that are of strategic importance to Beijing, helping increase resource extraction overseas. Additionally, the Bank extends more than 90 percent of its loans to state-owned companies, which themselves can engage in business ventures designed to support governmental rather than commercial ends. China's foreign aid programs, including concessional loans, are primarily controlled by the Ministries of Foreign Affairs, Finance, and Commerce, ensuring that foreign aid maximizes the benefits for China's state policies.[107] One example of this occurred during Chinese President Hu's visit to Africa, when he announced—while visiting the Merowe Dam project—that China had decided to write off more than $80 million in debt owed to it by Sudan.[108]

Major Loans by China Exim Bank to the Government of Sudan		U.S. $ millions
1996	First Export-Import Bank credit to Government of Sudan	12
1997	Kajbar Dam	200
1999	Khartoum Refinery	60
2001	El Gaili Power Station	220
2003	Qarre I Power Station	149
2003	Merowe Dam	300
2004	Education loan	3
2004	Conference Hall	3.6
2007	Presidential Palace	12.9
2007	Aid Loan	40
2007	Infrastructure loan	77.4
	Total	**1077.9**

The China Exim Bank's concessional loans are questionable as pure development tools in two ways. First, they are disproportionately focused on countries with significant energy resources, and are not targeted at commercially nonviable development projects in the world's poorest countries. Second, these loans are used to link China closely with borrower countries; loans are frequently offered instead of foreign aid and then forgiven once China has successfully established favorable economic relations with the borrowing state.[109]

By providing concessional loans rather than direct aid, China can condition these loans with the requirement that contracts for a given project are awarded to Chinese firms.[110] Also, it can require that products purchased in connection with funded projects must be obtained from China.[111] In addition, Beijing's potential loan forgiveness creates an incentive for borrowers to improve their political and economic connections with China. This policy benefits China at the same time that it helps the borrowing government, as China earns the goodwill of its borrowers twice: once when it extends a loan on favorable terms and again when it forgives the loan.

Critics charge that China's use of concessional loans to advance its own goals rather than to finance the most needed development projects in other countries undermines recent African debt relief endeavors while risking future cycles of unsustainable debt burdens.[112] That concessional loans play a key role in China's foreign policy certainly raises the question of whether Beijing isn't more willing to overlook rights abuses caused by the China Exim Bank—financed projects.[113] In Sudan, it is clear that China Exim Bank is operating at the behest of the Chinese government, which is in turn funding abuses through the Bank's projects.

Oil may have drawn China to Sudan, but Chinese involvement in Sudan's economy has gone far beyond the development of oil fields. The concessional loans and non-oil infrastructure projects emphasize the extent to which China's support dominates the country's economy, and therefore enables the ruling regime's activities.

Arms

"Everyone knows that the weapons in Darfur come from different sources and over a long period of time and they are not from one country ... But I can say we have nothing to do with that."
　—Li Chengwen, Chinese Ambassador to Sudan

While violence on the ground in Darfur escalated, China's sales of small arms to the government of Sudan were on the rise as well. At the same time, China also transferred several packages of military aircraft, provided hundreds of military trucks, and continued to strengthen military ties with Khartoum. And since 2004, the year in which the U.N. first instituted a mandatory arms embargo on weapons transfers to Darfur, China has become not only Sudan's largest small arms provider, but also practically its sole provider, as other countries extricated themselves from arms sales to Khartoum. The government of Sudan's wherewithal to pay China for these weapons ironically came from China itself. China's huge appetite for oil from Sudan filled Khartoum's coffers, enabling Sudan to return the favor by buying Chinese arms.

Khartoum's increased military spending began in the late 1990s, when oil revenues from China started enriching the government of Sudan, and rose more than six-fold between 1997 and 2000. During this time, Khartoum was both actively prosecuting the North-South war and becoming internationally isolated due to its sponsorship of terror-ism.[114] This combination of perceived military need and friendlessness, combined with China's attraction to Sudan's petroleum reserves, paved the way for a partnership based heavily on the twin imperatives of oil and arms. That relationship continues today, despite two U.N. resolutions imposing progressively stricter arms embargos on weapons transfers to Darfur and credible reports documenting Chinese arms in Darfur.

Small Arms Sales

In the last few years Sudan has aggressively pursued small arms of the sort used in Darfur. Trade data reported by Sudan to the United Nations, illustrated in the chart below, shows that Sudan's purchases of small arms, small arms parts, and ammunition have risen dramatically since 1999, the year that oil exports first flowed from the country. Small arms expenditures by Khartoum tripled from 1999 to 2000, then quadrupled in 2001, and climbed fifteen-fold in 2002. Sudan's small arms expenditures tripled again in 2003, dropped by one-third in 2004, and rose in 2005 to near the 2003 record high. By 2005, Sudan's small arms imports had risen to more than 680 times their 1999 levels. [115]

Experts generally agree that the worst violence in Darfur commenced in 2003, by which time China was providing small arms to Sudan valued in excess of $3 million. From that year to 2006 (the latest year in which small arms data is available), China sold over $55 million worth of small arms to Khartoum. Starting in 2004—the year in which the

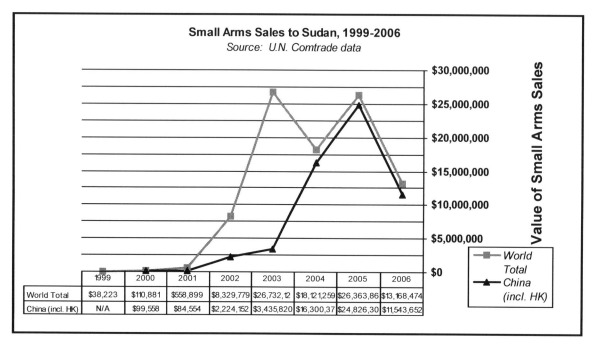

Small Arms Sales to Sudan, 1999-2006
Source: U.N. Comtrade data

	1999	2000	2001	2002	2003	2004	2005	2006
World Total	$38,223	$110,881	$558,899	$8,329,779	$26,732,12	$18,121,259	$26,363,86	$13,168,474
China (incl. HK)	N/A	$99,558	$84,554	$2,224,152	$3,435,820	$16,300,37	$24,826,30	$11,543,652

U.N. imposed an arms embargo—China sold Khartoum on average 90% of its small arms, and continued to be the near-exclusive provider through 2006.

These amounts are likely to be less than the true volume of weapons being transacted. If some of these weapons are sold at a discount to Sudan in order to make oil transactions with Chinese companies more attractive, Sudan could be buying a higher number of Chinese small arms than is documented by the U.N.[116] Regardless of the precise numbers, it is clear that China is selling the vast majority of small arms to Sudan at a time when other countries have ceased to do so.

Aircraft and Heavy Weapons

"Images from the parade have revealed to the world that the Sudanese army resembles a second Chinese Liberation Army."

—A defense analyst describing television footage from a military parade celebrating Sudan's 52nd Independence Day in 2007

Historically, China has not been Sudan's largest supplier of major weapons systems.[117] That title belongs to Russia, which is estimated to have provided almost three-quarters of imports for Sudan's current heavy military arsenal.[118] Since 2000, Russian weapons sales to Sudan have included a dozen MiG-29S attack aircraft (the most advanced in Sudan's air force), more than fifteen Mi-24P helicopter gunships, and at least sixty modern armored personnel carriers (APCs).[119]

Nonetheless, China's long history of selling military aircraft and heavy weapons transfers to Sudan is important for two reasons: first, because the early heavy weapons transactions laid the groundwork for the subsequent trade in small arms; and second, because China's heavy arms significantly enhance Khartoum's capacity to wage war in Darfur. Heavy arms transfers between China and Sudan date back decades, long before oil elevated Sudan's importance in Chinese eyes. China began selling advanced aircraft to the Sudanese government in the late 1960s, when it provided Khartoum an estimated 18 Mig-17 fighter jets.[120] In the 1970s, China sold Sudan approximately 130 tanks. And in the 1980s, Chinese military sales to Sudan included more than 20 fighter aircraft, 50 armored personnel carriers, and 50 towed artillery pieces.[121]

The first export of fighter aircraft from China to Sudan since Bashir's 1989 coup took place in 1997, the year CNPC began developing its first Sudanese oil fields. According to a database maintained by the Stockholm International Peace Research Institute (SIPRI), China delivered six or seven F-7M fighter aircraft to Sudan in 1997, the only documented major weapons purchase by the Sudanese that year.[122] These planes were far from cutting-edge at the time, but the benefit of the transaction to the Sino-Sudanese relationship may have far exceeded its military value.

China has continued to sell its military aircraft to Sudan since the outbreak of the Darfur conflict. In 2003, China sold up to 20 A-5C Fantan fighter-bombers to Sudan.[123] The Fantan is capable of delivering 4,000 pounds of bombs in a single strike. Although it is unclear how and where Sudan has used the Chinese jets, that same year, Khartoum was accused of dispatching its air force to bomb villages as part of its effort to wipe out the rebellion in Darfur.

In 2005, U.N. experts reported that the Chinese company Dongfeng exported more than two hundred military trucks to Sudan that year. Just two months later, new trucks of a similar type were found on a Sudanese air force base in Darfur. While the U.N. sought to determine whether these were the same trucks, and to determine the trucks' final destination, the Sudanese government failed to reply to a request for clarification on the origin of the trucks.[124] Reports from Darfur indicate that military trucks have been

used to transport Sudanese soldiers within the region, including to sites where civilians have been attacked.[125]

Another transfer came in 2006, when China reportedly delivered six K-8 advanced trainer aircraft, which can be fitted for ground attack combat, to Sudan.[126] That year, Khartoum continued to be accused of indiscriminate aerial bombing campaigns in Darfur and China stood accused of preventing action to stop them. More recently, television footage from a military parade celebrating Sudan's 52nd Independence Day in 2007 showed that Sudan had late-model battle tanks, infantry fighting vehicles, and military trainers from China.[127] In the words of a defense analyst, "Images from the parade have revealed to the world that the Sudanese army resembles a second Chinese Liberation Army."[128] According to the same analyst, Sudan is currently in negotiations with China for the purchase of 12 Chinese FC1 Fighter aircraft.[129]

Arms Sales During the U.N. Embargo

A U.N. embargo, initially imposed in 2004, expanded in 2005, and in effect to the present day, legally prevents all member states from selling or transferring arms or armaments to Darfur.[130] Despite the fact that Chinese arms have been well-documented in Darfur, the government of China has variously either disavowed their existence, minimized the scope of China's arms trade with Sudan, or simply denied that its weapons make a difference in the conflict. China's refusal to cease arms exports under these circumstances to Sudan indicates the greater significance of that aspect of its relationship with Khartoum. Beijing has used arms exports to help it both to enter and to stay in Sudan's oil markets.[131] China has more direct interests in selling arms to Sudan as well. Perhaps most importantly, China's arms sales help to return to China some of the funds used to purchase Sudanese oil.[132]

In 2004, U.N. Security Council resolution 1556 imposed a mandatory embargo on weapons transfers to Darfur, which was binding upon all member states including China and Sudan.[133] The U.N. embargo initially was limited to transfers of arms to "all nongovernmental entities and individuals" and only to those actors that were operating in a restricted geographic area: "the states of North Darfur, South Darfur and West Darfur." In March 2005, Security Council resolution 1591 extended the embargo to transfers of arms to the Sudanese armed forces operating in that area.[134] A Panel of Experts was also created at that time to monitor the situation in Darfur, including adherence to the arms embargo. China abstained from the vote on both resolutions, but is nonetheless bound by the embargo under international law. The embargo remains in place today.[135]

rifles and heavy machine guns.[136] Chinese officials initially denied that China was selling weapons to Sudan in spite of the embargo.[137] However, they have more recently been forced to admit that sales continue, but say the transfers are minor and that the weapons do not end up in Darfur. In 2007, when asked if China was worried that its arms were being used in Darfur, Li Chengwen, China's ambassador to Sudan, demurred. "Everyone knows that the weapons in Darfur come from different sources and over a long period of time and they are not from one country," he said. "But I can say we have nothing to do with that."[138] According to

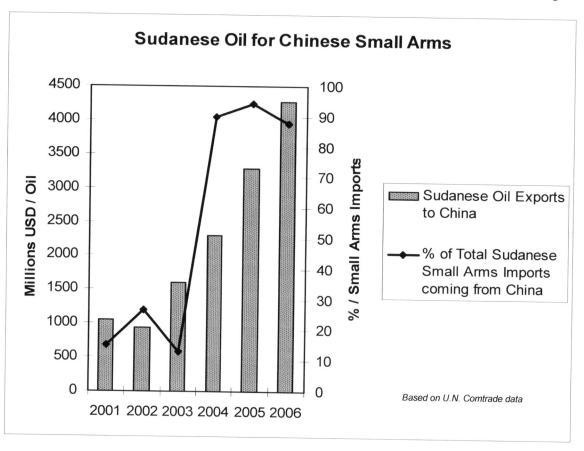

Sudanese Oil for Chinese Small Arms

Based on U.N. Comtrade data

Chinese sales of arms and military equipment to Sudan since 2004 have been extensive and observers on the ground in Darfur have reported seeing Chinese weaponry, including grenade launchers and ammunition for assault

Chinese Special Representative on Darfur Liu Guijin, "China has applied strict criteria in exporting weapons to Sudan ... and is not a major exporter [to the country]."[139]

A Chinese Foreign Ministry spokeswoman also defended Beijing's weapons exports, stating that "in conducting arms sales to Africa, we carefully consider the local area's situation and development model and stick to the spirit of protecting local peace and stability." The same spokeswoman indicated that it is Chinese policy not to sell arms to regions subject to U.N. Security Council arms embargoes, and that transferring Chinese weapons from buyers to third parties is not permitted.[140]

Khartoum, however, has openly stated its refusal to abide by the arms embargo, claiming that it is its "sovereign right to transfer weapons ... into Darfur."[141] The embargo is legally binding upon Sudan as a member of the U.N. and prohibits Khartoum from transferring weapons to its troops—whether government or militia—in Darfur. Faced with Sudan's defiance of its obligations, China's continued weapons sales to the government of Sudan, knowing that those weapons have been found in Darfur, put China in the position of also failing to comply with the embargo. Denying the extent of the transfers is not sufficient— the only way for China to ensure that it adheres to the arms embargo is to cease arms transfers until the violence in Darfur stops.

Chinese arms export law also emphasizes that exports must adhere to certain principles, including the requirement that they not cause "injury to the peace, security, and stability of the region concerned."[142] By this standard, Chinese arms transfers to Sudan are also in violation of its own domestic law. Stopping those transfers is the surest way for China to follow its own rules. However, China can do more. Its arms export law does not currently list respect for human rights or humanitarian law as a pre-condition to arms transfers to third countries.[143] China should amend this law so that its arms are no longer being used by governments and militias in carrying out mass atrocity crimes.

Military Cooperation

"Military relations between China and Sudan have developed smoothly ... China is further willing to develop cooperation between the two militaries in every sphere."

—Cao Gangchuan, Chinese Defense Minister, after an April 2007 meeting between the chief of staff of the Sudanese armed forces and the chief of general staff of China's People's Liberation Army (PLA)

China has not limited its support to bullets, shells and the means to shoot them. It also offers military expertise. China and Sudan have had extensive high-level military exchanges and China has assisted Sudan with the development of its domestic arms manufacturing sector.

In recent years, Chinese and Sudanese military leaders have participated in a series of high-level meetings. In March 2002, a Chinese military delegation headed by a senior military official visited both the Sudanese armed forces chief of staff and the Sudanese defense minister. Subsequently, no fewer than five high-level exchanges between Beijing and Khartoum occurred from 2003 to 2007, attended by the top-ranking officials of the Sudanese and Chinese armed forces.[144] Several of these visits occurred during the period of heaviest violence in Darfur.

An October 2005 meeting between Chinese military commanders and the Sudanese minister of national defense resulted in a plan for China to improve Sudan's armed forces.[145] More recently, an April 2007 meeting between the chief of staff of the Sudanese armed forces and the chief of general staff of China's People's Liberation Army (PLA) led to additional promises to increase cooperation between the two countries' militaries.[146] Chinese Defense Minister Cao Gangchuan asserted after this meeting that "military relations between China and Sudan have developed smoothly." He went on to indicate that "China is further willing to develop cooperation between the two militaries in every sphere."[147]

Support for Sudan's Arms Manufacturing Industry

While information about Chinese technical assistance to Sudan's domestic arms manufacturing sector is limited, Sudan could not have developed its domestic production in recent years without significant external support. President Bashir's claim that Sudan has become entirely self-sufficient in conventional arms production since the commencement of western economic sanctions is impossible to verify but is at odds with the massive conventional arms imports flowing into Sudan over the last few years.[148]

Chinese companies assisted the Sudanese government in establishing three assembly plants for small arms and ammunition outside Khartoum, located at Kalakla, Chojeri, and Bageer.[149] These factories are said to produce heavy and light machine guns, rocket launchers, mortars, antitank weapons, and ammunition.[150] In addition, one account of the Giad industrial complex near Khartoum—which includes military factories that produce tanks, military vehicles, and small arms, and which has been sanctioned by the U.S. government for its involvement in attacks in Darfur[151]—indicated that Chinese engineers were supervising the facility's work.[152]

On a smaller but no less dangerous scale, China also has either exported ammunition for Chinese-manufactured assault rifles and heavy machine guns in use by all parties to the violence in Darfur, or likely assisted with the development of a domestic Sudanese manufacturing base for such ammunition. In its final report, the U.N. Security Council's Panel of Experts established to monitor the Darfur arms embargo found evidence that suggested that "most ammunition currently used by parties to the conflict in Darfur is manufactured either in the Sudan or in China."[153]

China also contributes indirectly to the effectiveness of Sudan's armed forces through its construction of roads and airstrips that, while designed to allow the transport of oil and machinery, also permit Sudanese armed forces to travel more quickly throughout the oil-producing region.[154] These roads and airstrips, as well as refueling facilities located at oilfields operated by the GNPOC, were used by Sudanese military units engaging in attacks on civilians during the North-South civil war.[155]

China's roles as Sudan's primary provider of small arms, a major supplier of advanced weapons systems, and Khartoum's most powerful military partner cannot be divorced from the political and economic relationships between the two countries. Sudan's purchases of Chinese arms and China's support for Sudan's arms industry provide direct economic benefits to China and help keep the Bashir regime in power. Along with the bilateral training and exchanges, they also strengthen political ties between the two countries. The close political relationship between China and Sudan enables each government to obtain political backing from the other when they most need it.

China's Motivations

China has several reasons for wanting Khartoum to remain well armed. For one, arms sales provide Khartoum with an incentive to keep giving China preferential access to its oil.[156] Beijing has reportedly used arms exports to Sudan, a country under bilateral as well as U.N. embargo by many other arms-producing countries, to "sweeten" oil extraction deals with Chinese companies and thereby help them enter Sudan's oil markets. Such a coupling of arms sales and oil investment has expanded significantly in recent years, and the two countries' military relationship, established nearly four decades ago, has intensified with the growth of Chinese investment in Sudan's resources sector. China may also offset its enormous payments for Sudanese petroleum by providing arms to Sudan.[157]

Second, Africa is a significant market for arms exports from China: sales to African governments made up nearly one-quarter of all Chinese arms exports from 1998-2001 and more than 16 percent from 2002-2005.[158] While China is not the largest country of origin for international arms sales, Chinese arms exports to Africa constituted more than one-sixth of all arms transfers to the continent from 1998-2005.[159] As a country continuously at war with itself for many decades, Sudan is considered a valuable customer.

China has not historically been Sudan's largest supplier of major weapons systems—as noted above, that role belongs to Russia[160]—but China today is Sudan's single largest known provider of small arms.

Third, much of the weaponry that China sells to Sudan is not the latest generation; in some cases, the weapons systems have long been replaced by China's armed forces. Selling these weapons to Sudan therefore also reduces the costs of maintaining military equipment that was developed to counter a largely obsolete Soviet/Russian threat.[161]

Finally, having spent millions of dollars to build Sudan's energy infrastructure, China has a lot to lose: its oil-field crews could be attacked, its pipelines blown up, and its oil storage tanks burned. Many of China's oil facilities are located in the border areas, squarely astride the front lines of any renewed North-South conflict. According to one Chinese diplomat, China asked Khartoum in 2004 to send Sudanese security forces to oil-producing regions[162] and unconfirmed reports suggest that China contributes to both arming and training those troops.[163] More recently, China directly requested that Sudan provide protection for Chinese staff working on oil wells and other infrastructure projects after the Darfur Justice and Equality Movement (JEM) allegedly kidnapped two foreign oil workers.[164]

Under the Comprehensive Peace Agreement (CPA), security for oil installations in South Sudan is to be provided by joint North-South military forces, called Joint Installation Units (JIUs). However, this provision of the CPA is one of the many that have not yet been implemented, and the JIUs have not yet been formed. According to the U.N. Mission in Sudan (UNMIS), a high concentration of Sudanese armed forces remain in the areas surrounding the oil fields. Khartoum-supported "special police' or "oil police"—numbering approximately 3,000 and armed with approximately 4,000 small arms—have also been deployed near oil facilities.[165] Chinese oil blocks are also reportedly receiving protection from militias left over from the North-South civil war which are now being supported by Khartoum. One of these is said to be a branch of the South Sudan Defense Force (SSDF) led by former SPLM com-

mander Gordon Kong,[166] which now reportedly receives funding by Khartoum.

The continued presence of Sudanese armed forces and militias in the oil regions demonstrates the weak enforcement of key provisions of the CPA. It also constitutes a threat to peace in the region. An UNMIS official described Khartoum's deployment of those forces as "questionable," adding that local Southern Sudanese officials report the use of "oil police" to break up community demonstrations against oil companies that have contracted with Khartoum.[167]

Whether or not the Chinese government or state-owned companies offer direct support for these security forces, China's interest in protecting its oil installations is likely a motivating factor in its military cooperation with Sudan. And whatever its motivations for selling arms to Sudan, China's refusal to acknowledge the consequences of those sales to a regime that has been at war for decades defies credulity. China may officially insist on seeing the arms transfers in only economic terms, but the transfers link the government of China and the government of Sudan in more than economic ways.

Politics

"We do appreciate the support that China has given us in the Security Council."

—Omar al-Bashir, President of Sudan

China has repeatedly blocked action on the part of the international community, either by using its veto power in the United Nations Security Council, by voting against resolutions in human rights commissions, or by blocking action by the International Criminal Court.

Protecting Khartoum

The U.N. Security Council awakened to the Darfur conflict in 2004 and since then has taken largely ineffective steps to address it. The Security Council is the only U.N. body with the power to issue binding orders to any country. It has been limited in harnessing that power to resolve the crisis in Darfur by China's obstructionism. Since the U.N. commenced its efforts in 2004, China has sought to protect Sudan from intrusive measures such as broad economic sanctions. Sudan has exploited China's protection, engaging in a pattern of obfuscation, delay, and non-cooperation with the U.N. But for China, U.N. action might have resulted in better, earlier humanitarian intervention for the people of Darfur and tens of thousands of lives saved.

In 2004, China succeeded in watering down the language of Security Council resolution 1556, the Security Council's first serious response to the crisis. The United States and others lobbied vigorously to retain an explicit threat of comprehensive sanctions in the event that Sudan failed to disarm and prosecute Janjaweed who were accused of atrocities.[168] But China threatened a veto and successfully lobbied to weaken the text, including the removal of sanctions. Even after these changes were made, China abstained from voting. In explaining his country's position, Zhang Yishan, deputy permanent representative of China to the United Nations, argued that threatening to take coercive measures against the government of Sudan would not help the situation and would likely "complicate" the issue.[169]

Later that year, the Security Council again felt compelled to act on Darfur when the violence continued unabated, and China again successfully opposed the inclusion of specific coercive measures and forced their removal. Even with this weakened text, China abstained from the final vote. Explaining his country's opposition to the threat of economic penalties, Wang Guangya, China's permanent representative at the United Nations, noted that "it is our consistent view that instead of helping solve complicated problems, sanctions may make them even more complicated."[170] In his remarks on the resolution a few days after its passage, Sudanese President Bashir thanked "the true friends who stood up in the face of the unfair draft resolution," giving special praise to China and the three other countries that abstained from voting on the resolution—Algeria, Pakistan, and Russia.[171] As 2004 came to a close, Sudan's North-South peace process was in its final stages and the Security Council drafted resolution 1574, which focused primarily on the terms of the North-South peace agreement. But several members of the Security Council, partly as a result of pressure from nongovernmental organizations, wanted to use the special sitting as an opportunity to address the situation in Darfur.[172] China, Pakistan, Russia, and Algeria again opposed this move, arguing that taking tough action on Darfur might disrupt the North-South peace process.[173]

Throughout February and March 2005, political wrangling over Sudan continued at the Security Council. A number of countries including the United States continued to push for comprehensive sanctions on the government of Sudan. The original draft of resolution 1591 contained an explicit threat of an oil embargo against Khartoum in the event of continued noncompliance with the Security Council's demands. China again threatened to use its veto if the language was not changed, and again the automatic imposition of sanctions was changed to a statement that the Council would "consider taking" additional measures. And again, after insisting on the removal of the provision most threatening to Sudan—and China's own interests—China abstained from the vote.[174]

Among other measures, resolution 1591 called for a committee comprising Security Council members to designate persons meriting sanctions, and a four-member Panel of Experts to monitor the situation in Sudan and make recommendations on those people to the committee. Delays in the appointment of this Panel may have been due, in part, to China's rejection of candidates. In one instance, Beijing reportedly objected to a Briton who was "too critical of Sudan."[175]

China's involvement on resolution 1593, in which the Security Council referred the situation in Darfur to the International Criminal Court (ICC),[176] is interesting for its illustration of China's calculation of how far it could go to protect Sudan. China reportedly did not threaten to veto this resolution, a result of Beijing's belief that doing so would have carried too high a political cost, given the gravity of the crimes in question.[177] Moreover, China could not have shielded those Sudanese accused of war crimes

from all prosecutions, as the debate at the Security Council focused on whether the ICC or an ad-hoc tribunal would be the most appropriate forum—not whether prosecutions were appropriate.

From 2004, when the Security Council started to address the situation in Darfur, to the end of October 2007, the Security Council drafted and voted on fourteen substantive resolutions relating to Darfur.[178] In those resolutions, China insisted on removing tough language either criticizing Khartoum or subjecting it to sanctions on at least nine occasions, and of those, China abstained from voting on the resolution five times.[179] Three resolutions were introduced within the past year, and of those, China succeeded in watering down language at least twice. China still claims that it has played a productive role in helping to resolve the crisis.[180]

Obstruction in Other Fora

In other world fora, such as the now-defunct Commission on Human Rights and its successor, the Human Rights Council, no nation wields a veto that can thwart expressions of collective anger. Nonetheless, China historically endeavored to protect Sudan's actions from serious scrutiny or criticism in these fora—even before Darfur appeared in the international consciousness—and has refused to vote in favor of resolutions that criticize Khartoum.

Several times since 2000, the Commission on Human Rights adopted resolutions critical of the Khartoum government's role in human rights abuses in Sudan. Each time, China either voted against the resolution or abstained from the vote. It also consistently sought through its public statements to counter criticism of Sudan. These statements repeated China's view that the international community was not giving Khartoum enough credit for its efforts to improve human rights conditions, and that criticism of Sudan's human rights record was counterproductive. Beijing took a similar line when, in 2001, the General Assembly's Third Committee—responsible for oversight of social, humanitarian, and economic issues, including human rights—approved a draft resolution on human rights in Sudan. China voted against the resolution.[181] As it did before the Commission on Human Rights, China's delegate asserted that Sudan, far from being criticized, should be commended for its efforts to promote and protect human rights.

Months after the Human Rights Council replaced the Commission on Human Rights in 2006, the Council finally approached the issue of Darfur. In September 2006, the U.N. special rapporteur on the situation of human rights in Sudan, Sima Samar, presented a report to the Human Rights Council addressing the severe human rights abuses then underway in Darfur.[182] Zhang Yi, China's representative to the Human Rights Council, stated that China had faith in the Sudanese government's initiatives—including its cooperation with the special rapporteur and its attempts to improve the human rights situation—and urged the Council to take note of Khartoum's efforts on these fronts.[183]

In late 2006, the Human Rights Council adopted a decision on Darfur noting the seriousness of human rights violations and humanitarian crisis there and calling on the parties to stop the abuses. While China voted in favor of this decision, it voted against language noting Sudan's responsibility to protect people from such violations and the importance of bringing perpetrators to justice.[184] This language was kept out of the decision. Several western states voted against the resolution in protest at the extent to which China and others had watered it down.

China continued to try to strike a diplomatic balance at the Council when, with China's blessing, the Human Rights Council decided to dispatch a high-level mission to Darfur to assess the situation there. China's representative to the Council expressed his enthusiasm for the consensus decision and welcomed the support of African countries on the issue.[185] However, China later joined with other states in objecting to the report this high-level mission produced, supporting Khartoum's position that the mission had been procedurally flawed, and insisting that the substance of the report not be discussed.[186]

Thwarting the International Criminal Court

"A junior employee doing cheap work."

> — Zubair Bashir Taha, Sudanese Interior Minister, describing the Prosecutor of the International Criminal Court and the Court's investigation of war crimes and crimes against humanity in Darfur

Thus far, China has shielded Sudanese officials from accountability for crimes committed in Darfur. The political protection China has provided Sudan affects the international community's ability to address mass atrocities both in Darfur and elsewhere, because it challenges the integrity of the International Criminal Court (ICC).

On March 31, 2005, the U.N. Security Council referred the situation in Darfur to the prosecutor of the International Criminal Court. The Security Council's resolution 1593 officially authorized the prosecutor to start an investigation into the crimes allegedly committed in Darfur since mid-2002, and was legally binding on all member states of the United Nations, including Sudan. After 20 months of independent investigation, the prosecutor found reasonable evidence that Colonel Ali Mohammed Harun and Ali Mohamed Ali Abdel Rahman were responsible for war crimes and crimes against humanity committed in Darfur between 2003 and 2004. On the basis of the prosecutor's evidence, ICC judges issued international arrest warrants against Mohamed Harun and Ali Abdel Rahman in April 2007.

Khartoum called the ICC prosecutor a "junior employee doing cheap work," and has refused to accept the jurisdiction of the Court.[187] Sudan denies that mass crimes have been committed in Darfur and, in any event, insists that its own judiciary is competent to deal with whatever has occurred in the area. Sudanese authorities refuse to hand suspects over to the ICC.

Both Harun and Abdel Rahman are free to move about as they please within Sudan and it is unlikely that their alleged crimes in Darfur will ever be investigated by the highly politicized Sudanese judiciary. Harun, as Sudan's minister of state for humanitarian affairs, has authority over the refugee camps created as a direct consequence of his allegedly criminal activities in Darfur. Khartoum appointed Harun to head a commission charged with investigating human rights violations in Sudan and supervising the United Nations/African Union peacekeeping force in Darfur. And in January, Harun was promoted to adviser to the Ministry of Federal Affairs, which manages the government's relations with provinces outside Khartoum—such as Darfur. Sudanese authorities held Ali Abdel Rahman in custody for a short period on "suspicion of violating Sudanese laws" for crimes committed in Darfur, but released him in early October 2007 due to lack of evidence.

Though it "deplore[d] deeply the violations of international humanitarian law and human rights law and believe[d] that the perpetrators must be brought to justice," China abstained from voting on Security Council resolution 1593 authorizing such investigations. In explaining the vote, China indicated that it would prefer that justice be obtained in Sudanese courts. China is not a party to the Rome Statute creating the International Criminal Court. During negotiations on the Rome Statute, China opposed the Court's jurisdiction over war crimes or crimes against humanity committed during internal conflict. Nevertheless, as a permanent member of the Security Council, China has a responsibility to ensure that binding decisions made by the Council are respected, even if it abstained from the decision.

In September 2007, the Chinese ambassador to Sudan was photographed with Ahmad Harun at a gathering in Khartoum marking the transport of Chinese aid materials to Darfur. At the event, Harun thanked the Chinese government for its support, which he said indicated "the depth and solidity of the relations between Sudan and China." According to Chinese government media Xinhua, Harun also claimed that thanks to the support of Sudan's friends, the Darfur cause was moving steadily forward towards a "final solution."[188] As this photo-op demon

strated, the government of Sudan has no better friend than China in its quest to hold on to power and extract wealth, no matter the consequences to the people it governs.

Mixed Messages

However cynical the September 2007 gathering was, the delivery of Chinese aid was one of several small signs that Beijing might finally be troubled by the disaster in Darfur, or at least by its association with the regime responsible. In May 2006, a seventh round of peace talks ended with the signing of the Darfur Peace Agreement (DPA). The DPA seemed to create a new window for peace and provided a new impetus to put a strong peacekeeping presence on the ground.

Though weaknesses in the DPA became apparent immediately, troops in Darfur now fly the U.N. flag. The presence of U.N. troops is due in part to China's increasing willingness in the past year to use its influence to urge Khartoum to accept the deployment of a U.N. peacekeeping force for Darfur. But whether China will continue to play such a role—especially in situations in which less international pressure is brought to bear on Beijing—remains to be seen. Chinese Special Representative Liu claimed "the Chinese side has made a huge effort … . The Chinese side has utilized all kinds of channels and talked to the Sudanese government and persuaded them as an equal partner … ."[189] However, that effort appears to be limited to what looks to the international community to be gentle private discussion, with the occasional public comment when absolutely necessary; stronger action such as sanctions remains off the table.

The diplomatic wrangling over the past two years provides a window into the development of Chinese policy on Darfur. From the start, Khartoum expressed opposition to a proposed U.N. peacekeeping force for Darfur, citing fears of western, neo-imperialist occupation. Sudan continued this opposition at every step of the planning process and embarked on a large scale diplomatic campaign to persuade other states to agree.[190] As a result, in March 2006, the African Union (A.U.) Peace and Security Council voted to extend the African Union Mission in Sudan (AMIS) for an additional 6 months, and supported "in principle" the transition to a U.N. force with the acceptance of the government of Sudan.[191]

Chinese Ambassador Zhang Yishan explained that, in light of the A.U.'s endorsement, China was willing to support a Security Council resolution establishing a U.N. peace-keeping force. However, Zhang expressed China's opposition to a Chapter VII mandate for the force[192] (authorizing troops to use force when necessary) and reportedly joined with Russia in attempts to remove the threat of sanctions from the text during negotiations.[193] In a subsequent draft, the U.S. and U.K., however, succeeded in overriding China's main objections and the resolution passed in late August, with a Chapter VII mandate for the force. China, along with Russia and Qatar, abstained in protest.[194]

Many saw the resolution as an empty promise. Sudan continued to hold the international community hostage by rejecting any possibility of a U.N. presence in Darfur. On a trip to Beijing soon after resolution 1706 was passed, Sudanese President Bashir said his country would not accept a U.N. force, and thanked his Chinese hosts for their support on the matter: "We do appreciate the support that China has given us in the Security Council ... [and thank them for] the[ir] (sic) insistence that the support of Sudan must be sought in any resolution that can be passed."[195] Sudan clearly recognized that with China's help, division in the Security Council was assured, enabling Khartoum to fend off truly coercive measures.

China began to come under intense public and diplomatic pressure to play an active role in the efforts to convince Sudan to accept the force after the passage of resolution 1706. Realizing that its hands-off approach to Darfur was becoming increasingly untenable in the face of the determination of others to act, China's Ambassador to the U.N. Wang Guangya reportedly played an instrumental role in convincing Sudan that the U.N.'s plans came with no hidden agenda.[196] Wang's persuasion

resulted in Sudan's acceptance, in principle at least, of the "Annan Plan," a three-stage process leading to the deployment of a hybrid U.N.-A.U. peacekeeping force for Darfur. However, Khartoum quickly showed that agreement in principle was no guarantee of action, and continued to find reasons to stall the process.

When Bashir finally agreed to the hybrid force, China was quick to take credit for Sudan's turnaround. Chinese Special Representative on Darfur Liu Guijin asserted that "from the highest leader in China to relevant foreign ministry officials, we have always used our method of using our words and made use of every opportunity and channel in every aspect of work, especially with the Sudanese government." Liu also said that he had personally conveyed to the Sudanese government his concerns about Chinese-made weapons being used by government-backed militias.[197] He further commented that western nations should stop doubting Sudan's intentions and be more welcoming of the steps forward.[198]

China's relationship with Sudan was publicly tested when President Bashir essentially reversed himself and withdrew Sudan's support for the hybrid force. China's reaction was calibrated: U.N. Ambassador Wang stated publicly that Bashir's response was not what China expected, but he also said that China remained opposed to the calls for renewed sanctions on Sudan being made by several council members.[199] At the China-Africa summit in Beijing in November 2006 and again when he visited Sudan in February 2007, President Hu Jintao reportedly encouraged President Bashir in private to allow the hybrid force to be deployed.[200] In April 2007, Chinese Foreign Minister Zhai Jun traveled to Sudan, visited refugee camps in Darfur, and met with Bashir in Khartoum. Zhai stated that China was "expecting more flexibility on the Annan plan," but simultaneously expressed appreciation for Sudan's efforts in restoring peace in Darfur.[201]

China continues to try to placate both its economic trading partner, Sudan, and the community of states of which it wants to be an accepted and esteemed member. In May 2007, Liu Guijin, formerly Chinese ambassador to

Zimbabwe and South Africa, was appointed Special Representative of the Chinese Government on the Darfur Issue. In making that unprecedented appointment, Beijing seemed to acknowledge that it could no longer ignore Darfur. One of Liu's first actions was to visit the region and to hold meetings in Khartoum.[202] Yet Liu remarked during his trip that the situation in Darfur appeared to be "largely stabilized"–a conclusion that was met with derision from activists and the media. Beijing also announced it would send an additional $10 million in humanitarian aid to Darfur[203] and would commit 275 military engineers to the first phase of the hybrid force, strengthening the African Union force already on the ground.[204]

In March 2007, China's National Development and Reform Commission removed Sudan from China's list of countries with preferred trade status, eliminating state subsidies and preferential treatment for Chinese investment in Sudan. The U.S. State Department and other observers lauded the move as an indication of China's willingness to use coercive economic measures to sway Khartoum.[205]

China's role was welcomed by the international community, including the United States. In response to a question regarding China's role in trying to resolve the Sudan crisis, U.S. Deputy Secretary of State John Negroponte called China's role "very constructive," given Beijing's "multifaceted relationship with the country of Sudan." Negroponte asserted that "the Chinese have helped us and the international community generally by conveying to the Government of Sudan the importance of it complying with the wishes and the mandates of the international community."[206]

Yet the Government of Sudan's consent to the deployment of the hybrid force was not the final obstacle to the deployment of the force. The U.N. now reports delays at every turn in the form of bureaucratic obstacles and objections to the force composition from Khartoum.[207] Sudan's obstruction became far more serious when, just over a week after the U.N. began deployment of its

peacekeepers, its military attacked a U.N. convoy, killing a Sudanese driver.[208]

China has continued to shield Sudan from international pressure. In December 2007, after the ICC Prosecutor reported to the Security Council that Sudan is failing to cooperate with his investigation, a majority of Security Council member states were in favor of issuing a strong statement urging Sudan to hand over the indicted suspects. According to diplomats from other member states, China insisted on changes to the statement that weakened it so much that other Council members decided not to issue it.[209]

Other facets of China's recent engagement with Sudan provide further evidence that Ambassador Negroponte's praise came too quickly. During his February 2007 visit to Sudan, President Hu canceled $80 million of Sudanese debt, announced a $1.2 billion railway reconstruction project, and granted a $50 million interest-free loan for the construction of a new presidential palace.[210]

China's claims to play a positive role in resolving the Darfur conflict will be borne out only if it exerts sufficient and consistent pressure on Khartoum to achieve real security in Darfur.

Looking Ahead: China's Courting of South Sudan

The Government of Southern Sudan (GOSS), established after the signing of the Comprehensive Peace Agreement (CPA) in 2005, has a complicated relationship with China. Perhaps realizing that exclusively supporting Khartoum might prove dangerous if Southern Sudan secedes—with its oil fields—after the 2011 referendum, Beijing has seemed keen to foster good relations with the interim government in Juba. Chinese oil concessions, concentrated in territory at least nominally controlled by GOSS, were negotiated by Khartoum before the CPA was signed. Southern Sudan has made clear its view that all oil concessions will be reviewed after the 2011 referendum, and both China and the GOSS seem to be preparing for such an eventuality.

Many GOSS leaders remain skeptical of Beijing's motives, due to China's economic, military, and political support for Khartoum during the 21-year civil war. China's history of supplying Khartoum with weapons, as well as vast oil revenue after 1999, is not lost on GOSS leaders. In the words of one source within the Government of Southern Sudan:

> "China is enemy number one—they are the ones who kept El Basher (sic) in power for so long, providing him with weapons to try and win the war in the South. They are the ones who supplied him with helicopter gun ships on the attacks on Bentiu and other places—they are evil. They are the ones who are providing military support to the government on Darfur—of course they are."[211]

Despite these misgivings, China's ties to Southern Sudan appear to be strengthening. The GOSS maintains significant budget deficits and continues to struggle financially, and sources indicate that senior leaders in Southern Sudan already receive financial backing from the Chinese.[212] Additionally, GOSS plans to construct a new pipeline from Southern Sudan to the Kenyan coast seem unlikely to be carried out and, as a result, Southern Sudan will be forced to continue to use Chinese-owned pipelines running from fields in Unity and West Upper Nile provinces to Port Sudan in the north.

Already, leaders from China and Southern Sudan have begun to cultivate relationships. In January 2005, the month that the CPA was adopted, leaders from Southern Sudan visited China at the invitation of the government.[213] Another delegation including Costello Garang, a SPLM/A special advisor and the chief negotiator for Southern Sudan on oil matters, visited Beijing in 2007.[214] Sources report that China has brought senior members of the SPLM/A to Beijing to discuss securing oil concessions in Southern Sudan.[215] Other investment opportunities have also been raised with the Chinese leadership, as SPLM leaders have made several trips to Beijing to discuss construction, telecommunications, housing, and road-building projects.[216] SPLM ministers have also joined delegations with NCP ministers to discuss economic matters as part of the Government of National Unity (GoNU).

These high-level visits have not been unilateral; the Chinese have visited Southern Sudan as well. When Hu Jintao visited Khartoum in February 2007, he met with Sudanese First Vice President and GOSS leader Salva Kiir in private, and the two reportedly spoke about the 2011 referendum. Kiir reportedly told Hu that China would have to negotiate with Southern Sudan directly for oil concessions, and that China would need to develop a strategy to deal with the post-2011 reality.[217] Months later, in July 2007, Kiir led a GoNU delegation to China which included Minister of Energy and Mining Awad el Jazz and Minister of Foreign Affairs Dr Lam Akol.[218] At least one other senior GOSS member did not join the group because, he said, "The president knows I can't stand the Chinese and want nothing to do with them."[219]

Despite the ambivalence of some South Sudanese officials, China's strategy of hedging its bets in Sudan seems to be yielding some concrete results. China's Export-Import Bank reportedly provided the GOSS with a $1 billion soft loan in 2006, though this has not appeared in the GOSS budget.[220] Chinese companies have engaged in negotiations with the GOSS directly related to telecommunications equipment contracts, the construction of the Juba-Mombasa railway, and a project to rebuild the Southern Sudan government assembly building in Juba.[221] More recently, a Chinese delegation visited Juba in August 2007, and the head of the delegation indicated that China is considering possibilities for development in Southern Sudan in the health, education, water supply, roads and bridges, and agriculture sectors.[222]

Conclusion

"Unless China does its part to ensure that the government of Sudan accepts the best and most reasonable path to peace, history will judge your government as having bank-rolled a genocide."
—Letter from 107 members of the U.S. House of Representatives to President Hu Jintao, May 9, 2007

To date, China has not paid much of a price for remaining close to Sudan. But while the oil continues to flow to the Chinese economy, there is real risk in the Chinese government's cynicism. To ensure the continuation of its economic boom, China needs stable markets and a guarantee that its investments are safe. But by consistently siding with a rogue regime in Khartoum, China puts such stability and guarantees in play. The government in Khartoum might not always be there to protect China's investments and needs, especially as it has a history of fomenting conflict. How the next leaders might feel about China's role is uncertain at best.

What might start to turn Beijing's attitudes would not be mere words, but economic reprisals and public shame. Loss of income would hit China where it is most vulnerable. According to a May 15 regulatory filing, Boston-based Fidelity Investments sold at least 38 percent of the 1.1 billion shares it held in PetroChina after Massachusetts legislators urged it to cut ties to China because of its Sudan policies. The upcoming Olympic Games offer another opportunity for pressure: not only would China lose money if tourists and nations stayed away from the Olympics, but those games would no longer be a grand validation of Chinese success. They would be a reminder of what China has not done for Darfur. Legislators, entertainers and other activists have publicly raised the specter of such a boycott if China does not begin to use its unique sway with Khartoum.

Talk of a boycott, no matter how remote the likelihood, seems to have rattled China. Since early January, its special representative for Darfur repeatedly has claimed that tying Darfur to the Olympics was unfair, because China cannot be held responsible for what Sudan does. He added that China has already used its influence to urge Sudan to accept a peacekeeping force. But if Beijing wants admiration at the Olympics, it must do far more to stop the suffering in Darfur. As members of the U.S. Congress wrote to Chinese President Hu Jintao recently, "Unless China does its part to ensure that the government of Sudan accepts the best and most reasonable path to peace, history will judge your government as having bank-rolled a genocide." What China is missing is a sense of urgency—an urgency that matches its urgent quest for oil. Until China recognizes that its economic involvement in countries has strong political consequences—that it is in fact already interfering in other countries' domestic political matters by throwing its economic weight around—the world will see China as an enabler of atrocities, not as an Olympic-sized success.

Recommendations to the Government of China

Terminate Arms Transfers and Military Training in Darfur

1. China should immediately terminate arms transfers to all parties involved in the conflict in Darfur, including the Sudanese government, to ensure that the embargo imposed by Security Council resolutions 1556 (2004) and 1591 (2005) is fully implemented. China also should immediately terminate any other form of military support to the Sudanese government, including training activities.

2. China should support the expansion of the U.N. Security Council arms embargo on Darfur to the whole of Sudan and prohibit the sale and supply of arms and related materiel to non-state armed groups located in or operating from Chad.

3. China should pressure Sudan to immediately ratify and implement the Nairobi Protocol for the Prevention, Control and Reduction of Small Arms and Light Weapons in the Great Lakes Region and the Horn of Africa, to which Sudan is a signatory. In particular, China should demand that the Sudanese government adopt national legislation criminalizing violations of U.N. arms embargoes and prohibiting civilian possession and use of small arms, as required by Article 3 of the Nairobi Protocol.

4. China should amend the "Regulations of the People's Republic of China on Administration of Arms Exports" to prohibit the transfer of arms to countries where they may or will be used for violations of international humanitarian law and human rights law.

5. China should institute a robust, enforceable "end-use certificate system" to ensure that any armaments transferred to third countries cannot be used in any manner contrary to international law.

Stop Shielding Sudan before International Institutions

6. China should refrain from using its veto or threat of veto in the Security Council to impede efforts to stop mass atrocities in Sudan and elsewhere. China should stop blocking resolutions that aim to impose sanctions on governments that commit mass atrocities when such resolutions would otherwise receive a majority of votes within the Security Council. China, furthermore, should stop weakening the language of Security Council resolutions that are critical of such governments.

7. China should stop shielding the human rights records of its trade partners within the United Nations in general and at the Human Rights Council in particular. China should vote in favor of any future resolution of the Human Rights Council condemning or aiming to end the human rights crisis in Sudan.

Support Peace, Justice and Accountability in Sudan

8. China should unreservedly support the ongoing efforts of the international community to institute a sustainable and inclusive peace process in Sudan. In particular, China should volunteer to provide technical and material assistance to the representatives of the various groups of civilians directly affected by the conflict, including women's groups, internally displaced persons and refugees, so as to facilitate their participation in the peace negotiations.

9. As a permanent member of the Security Council, China should use its influence to guarantee that the African Union/United Nations peacekeeping operation (UNAMID), authorized by the Council, be deployed to Darfur immediately. China should urge the government of Sudan to accept unconditionally the composition of the operation proposed by the United Nations and to remove all legal, administrative, and practical impediments to troop deployment. Should Sudan continue to evade its legal obligations by obstructing the full and immediate deployment of UNAMID, China should support efforts in the U.N. Security Council to place targeted sanctions on key Sudanese government officials, including President Omar al-Bashir. Additionally, China should help fund and commit additional troops for the UNAMID operation and help supply the 24 transport and security helicopters needed by UNAMID to ensure that the mission can operate effectively.

10. China should publicly support efforts to hold individuals in Sudan accountable for committing mass atrocities at the International Criminal Court (ICC). Specifically, China should urge Sudan to immediately comply with the warrants issued by the ICC for the arrest of Ahmad Harun and Ali Kushayb and to surrender to the ICC these two individuals who face multiple charges of crimes against humanity and war crimes in Darfur. Should Sudan continue to evade its legal obligation to comply with the ICC arrest warrants, China should support efforts in the United Nations Security Council to place targeted sanctions on key Sudanese government officials, including President Omar al-Bashir.

Appendices

Appendix A

Protection and Money: A Timeline[223]

All sums given in U.S. Dollar

2004	International Action on Darfur	Chinese Dealings with Sudan
January		Foreign Minister Li Zhaoxing visits Sudan, signs several economic and other bilateral cooperation agreements.
May-June		CPECC (a CNPC subsidiary) wins two contracts, for construction of pipeline from Block 3 and 7 to Port Sudan and of the Beshair II marine terminal, worth a total of $405 million.[224]
June		China signs a U.S. $3.6 million preferential loan agreement with Khartoum for a new International Conference Hall as well as for training Sudan's Ministry of International Cooperation employees.[ ]
July	China abstains from voting on Security Council resolution 1556, even after insisting on the removal of a direct threat of sanctions and preventing the Council from creating a committee to monitor Sudan's compliance.[226]	China grants a U.S. $3 million loan to support technical education in Sudan; the money is used for construction of technical colleges.[ ]
September	China abstains from voting on Security Council resolution 1564, even after forcing the removal of an explicit threat of sanctions on Sudan's petroleum sector if Sudan failed to comply.[228]	
November	China is among the states that object to the inclusion of any significant action on Darfur in resolution 1574 on the North-South peace process.[229]	
2005	International Action on Darfur	Chinese Dealings with Sudan
March	China abstains from voting on resolution 1591 even after forcing the removal of the threat of an oil embargo in the event of continued noncompliance by Sudan.[230] China also abstains on resolution 1593 referring the situation in Darfur to the International Criminal Court (ICC),[231] saying that China could not endorse the exercise of the ICC's jurisdiction against the will of non-State parties."[232]	

July	The Panel of Experts created by resolution 1591 is finally named after 3 months of delays caused by Chinese objections to candidates, including one who China said was "too critical of Sudan."[233]	
August		The Chinese state-owned Harbin Power Equipment Company signs a U.S. $400 million contract to build seven substations and 1,776 km of transmission lines for the Merowe Dam[~]
CNPC buys 35% of the rights to Sudan's first offshore gas development in Block 15[~]
China agrees to donate $6 million in aid money for the construction of 80 primary and secondary school as well as building laboratories for 1,000 high schools in Southern Sudan[~]
2006	**International Action on Darfur**	**Chinese Dealings with Sudan**
April	China abstains from voting on resolution 1672, even after reducing the number of individuals targeted for sanctions from seventeen, including members of the Sudanese government and armed forces, to just four people, only one of whom was a member of the Sudanese armed forces.[237]	
May	China votes in favor of in resolution 1679 but expresses opposition to the invocation of Chapter VII in the text.[~] China had also unsuccessfully attempted to remove a threat of sanctions.[~]	
August-September	The Security Council adopts resolution 1706 authorizing a U.N. peacekeeping force for Darfur, despite China's attempts to delay the vote in order to first secure Sudan's consent to the deployment, and efforts to prevent the force being given a Chapter VII mandate.[~] China abstains from the vote in protest.[~]	
November	China's U.N. Ambassador is said to play a pro-active role in attempts to persuade Khartoum to accept a U.N. presence in Darfur at a high-level meeting in Addis Ababa.[~]
President Bashir visits Beijing for the Forum on China-Africa Cooperation and thanks China for its support at the Security Council.[243] President Hu reportedly encourages him in private to accept the U.N. in Darfur	.

2007	International Action on Darfur	Chinese Dealings with Sudan
January	U.S. Presidential Envoy to Sudan Andrew Natsios visits Beijing to push China to persuade Sudan to accept U.N. troops.	CNPC signs a U.S. $1 million donation agreement with the Sudanese Ministry of Welfare and Social Development to help improve the country's social system. The company signs another agreement with the Sudanese Ministry of Energy and Mining, under which the Chinese oil company will earmark U.S. $900,000 dollars to train Sudanese oil professionals.™
February	President Hu visits Sudan in February 2007 and again reportedly encouraged Bashir to allow the hybrid force to be deployed™.	The Sudanese government signs an agreement with China Railway Engineering Group Ltd and one of its conglomerates, Transtech Engineering for the upgrading of the railway line between Khartoum and the Port of Sudan.™ The contract is valued at U.S. $1.15 billion, making it the largest capital investment deal between the two countries to date.™ President Hu announces an interest free loan of $12.9 million for the construction of a new presidential palace, $40 million in aid loans, $77.4 million for infrastructure projects, and the elimination of up to $70 million in Sudanese debt.™
April	Chinese Foreign Minister Zhai Jun travels to Sudan, visits refugee camps in Darfur and meets with Bashir in Khartoum, telling him that China expects more flexibility.	
May	More than 100 members of the U.S. house of represen-tatives and a bipartisan group of Senators send letters to President Hu Jintao saying Beijing's 2008 Olympic Games could be affected if China doesn't do more to resolve the crisis in Darfur. China appoints Liu Giujin as its special representative for Darfur. Liu visits Darfur and holds meetings in Khartoum. Beijing announces an additional $10 million in Chinese aid to Darfur™ and a commitment of 275 military engineers to the first phase of the hybrid force.	The Chinese government and government of Sudan signed an agreement inaugurating an air cargo line between the two countries facilitating trade and direct commercial flights.[250]
June	Bashir unequivocally accepts the hybrid force in a letter to the U.N. Secretary General.	CNPC signs an agreement with the Sudanese government for a 35 percent to 40 percent stake in the development of Block 13 in the Red Sea.™
July	Security Council resolution 1769 passes, creating UNAMID, a joint United Nations-African Union mission in Darfur. China votes in favor of the resolution.	

| December | The prosecutor of the International Criminal Court reports to the Security Council that Sudan has failed to cooperate with his investigation. China obstructs efforts by a majority of Security Council member states to issue a strong statement urging Sudan to hand over the indicted suspects. | |

Appendix B

Background on Sudan: An Isolated Regime

In 1995, President Omar al-Bashir of Sudan traveled to Beijing to conclude the first oil exploration and production agreement between the two countries.[252] By that time, Sudan had been the scene of almost nonstop internal conflict since its independence from Great Britain in 1956. Bashir's Islamist government had been condemned by the United Nations and human rights groups for its deplorable human rights record. Sudanese armed forces and government-sponsored militias had committed massive abuses in the conflict in the southern region of the country.[253] Confirming its international pariah status, Bashir's regime was a known sponsor of international terrorism and had been on the U.S. State Department list of State Sponsors of Terrorism since 1993.[254]

The oil reserves that Bashir offered to China in 1995 had been discovered by U.S. oil giant Chevron in 1978, and were located in the region of southern Sudan. Since 1983, the rebel Sudan People's Liberation Army (SPLA) had fought to reclaim autonomy for the South, where the largely non-Muslim population objected to Khartoum's imposition of Shari'a (Islamic) law and the Arabic language. Undoubtedly, however, control of the region's oil wealth was a primary goal of both sides.

Southerners had good reason to doubt that they would be allowed to share in the spoils of oil extraction. In 1980, then President Nimeiri had attempted to redraw the North-South border to place the proven oilfields in Northern territory. After heavy resistance from the South, Nimeiri had planned to build a pipeline from the southern oil fields to Port Sudan, a northern city on the Red Sea. This pipeline would not have provided the South with any new infrastructure, and earnings from the exported oil would have been sent to Khartoum.[255]

That same year, Sudan's government armed a proxy militia force to evacuate villages around two of Chevron's newly-discovered oil fields in Upper Nile province.[256] These *murahaleen* (nomadic raiders), marginalized Arab cattle herders from western and northern Kordofan and Darfur provinces, were told that they could steal the cattle of those villages they attacked.[257] The government-backed *murahaleen* did more than that, burning and looting villages and forcing children into slavery. Khartoum's successful strategy of pitting different tribes, ethnicities, and religions against each other soon led to real tensions between these groups.[258]

The change of power from Nimeiri to Bashir in a 1989 coup brought no fundamental change of military strategy. Bashir's National Islamic Front government continued to organize and arm militias comprised of Arab tribes to fight against the rebels[259] and to forcibly expel, abduct, rob, and kill civilians in areas near Sudan's oil fields.[260]

After three of its employees were killed by Southern rebel attacks in 1984, Chevron suspended its operations in Sudan. Eight years later, still shut down by violence on the ground, the company was forced to sell its interest in Sudanese oil.[261]

Against this backdrop of violence, insecurity and international isolation, the China National Petroleum Corporation (CNPC) began developing Sudan's oil fields in 1996.

Since then, China has been a stalwart supporter of the Bashir regime despite its continued violent repression of its own citizens. In the same period, Sudan's international pariah status has only increased. In 1997, President Bill Clinton imposed comprehensive economic sanctions for Sudan's support of terrorism and record of human rights violations.[262] The U.N. Security Council imposed terrorism-related sanctions against Sudan in the late 1990s, but lifted them in 2001 once Sudan displayed its willingness to cease supporting terrorist groups.[263] The U.S. sanctions continued in force, however, and were expanded by the Bush Administration in response to the Sudanese government's role in the Darfur crisis.[264]

Such sanctions have discouraged or prohibited western companies from accessing Sudan's oil reserves, but they have not succeeded in completely cutting off financial support for the Khartoum government. They have therefore not succeeded in their ultimate goal—to convince the government to stop its atrocities. This may be due in part to mixed signals from western powers, including the U.S., which have maintained ties with the Sudanese intelligence services through counterterrorism efforts. But the failure has primarily come about because Sudan has earned approximately $2 billion annually from oil sales to China and other Asian countries, making it one of Africa's fastest growing economies. This oil revenue provides the hard currency that enables Khartoum to fund arms purchases and organize armed militias. As long as oil investors continue to fund Sudan's ability to commit atrocities, they impede the international community's efforts to pressure Khartoum to end the slaughter in Darfur, to implement the Comprehensive Peace Agreement (CPA) that ended the war with the South in 2005, and to generally to respect human rights within its borders.

The Conflict in Darfur

Darfur historically has been home to nomadic Arab tribes, who lived primarily in the region's dry north, and sedentary African agriculturalists and cattle herders, who tended to live in the region's south.[265] When droughts came in the 1980s, water, grassland, and arable soil became increasingly scarce and northern nomadic tribes began to spend more time on the region's southern farm lands,[266] creating conflicts over land and water.[267] In an earlier era, disputes such as these would have been resolved through negotiation by tribal elders. In the 1980s, however, the national government introduced new local governance structures prioritizing allegiance to Khartoum over community respect as the basis for leadership.[268] Khartoum's decision to arm tribal actors added to violence in Darfur, as disputes were increasingly settled with gunfire.

In 2003, as the North-South peace process was gaining momentum, the situation in Darfur quickly deteriorated with rebel groups taking up arms against the national government. The groups' grievances stemmed from Khartoum's neglect of the economically depressed Darfur region, its practice of awarding senior posts in the regional government to Arabs, and its refusal to include Darfur in the North-South agreements on wealth and power sharing.[269] Darfur's rebels, who were not party to the North-South peace talks, concluded that only through military action could they stake a claim in the country's new political and economic order.[270]

With an overextended military, Khartoum turned to a familiar strategy: arming nomadic Arab tribesmen eager to settle disputed territory and launching a proxy paramilitary war.[271] This new paramilitary force came to be known as the *Janjaweed*, or "men on horses with guns." While the Sudanese military bombed Darfuri villages from the air, the Janjaweed would attack with small arms from the ground—shooting and raping civilians, burning homes, and looting villages.[272]

Although Khartoum has repeatedly denied organizing and arming the Janjaweed, ample evidence exists to the contrary. The International Criminal Court (ICC) concluded there were reasonable grounds to believe the Janjaweed not only acted under the command of the Sudanese armed forces, but also received material and physical support from Khartoum.[273] By linking evidence of militia members' weaponry, vehicles, and uniforms to the government of Sudan, the U.N. Office of the High Commission for Human Rights concluded that "[g]overnment knowledge, if not complicity, in the attacks is almost certain."[274]

With presidential elections scheduled for 2009, Khartoum has some incentive to ensure that Darfur's rebels do not pose a threat to the National Congress Party's hold on power, and by extension, its ability to maintain control of the country's valuable oil resources. The 2011 referendum on the South's independence makes consolidating power even more important to Khartoum, which may need support from other regions—such as Darfur—if the South votes to secede, leading to the outbreak of war over the country's oil fields.[275]

In May 2006, Khartoum and one faction of the Sudanese Liberation Army/Movement (SLA/M) signed the Darfur Peace Agreement (DPA) under significant international pressure. Since then, the situation on the ground has only deteriorated. The DPA had little popular support and its terms are largely unfulfilled. New peace talks due to begin in Libya in October 2007 were delayed, ostensibly to allow the rebel groups time to prepare, but actually because many groups refused to attend.[276]

Appendix C

Map of Sudan

Source: United Nations Mission in Sudan

Appendix D

Map of Sudan's Oil Blocks

European Coalition on Oil in Sudan

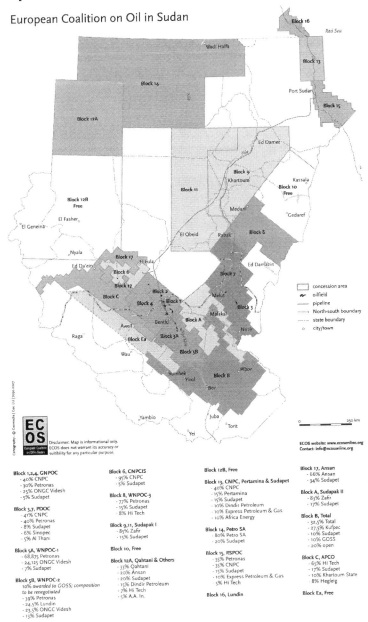

Block 1,2,4, GNPOC
- 40% CNPC
- 30% Petronas
- 25% ONGC Videsh
- 5% Sudapet

Block 3,7, PDOC
- 41% CNPC
- 40% Petronas
- 8% Sudapet
- 6% Sinopec
- 5% Al Thani

Block 5A, WNPOC-1
- 68.875 Petronas
- 24.125 ONGC Videsh
- 7% Sudapet

Block 5B, WNPOC-2
10% awarded to GOSS; composition
to be renegotiated
- 39% Petronas
- 24.5% Lundin
- 23.5% ONGC Videsh
- 13% Sudapet

Block 6, CNPCIS
- 95% CNPC
- 5% Sudapet

Block 8, WNPOC-3
- 77% Petronas
- 15% Sudapet
- 8% Hi Tech

Block 9,11, Sudapak I
- 85% Zafir
- 15% Sudapet

Block 10, Free

Block 12A, Qahtani & Others
- 33% Qahtani
- 20% Ansan
- 20% Sudapet
- 15% Dindir Petroleum
- 7% Hi Tech
- 5% A.A. In.

Block 12B, Free

Block 13, CNPC, Pertamina & Sudapet
- 40% CNPC
- 15% Pertamina
- 15% Sudapet
- 10% Dindir Petroleum
- 10% Express Petroleum & Gas
- 10% Africa Energy

Block 14, Petro SA
- 80% Petro SA
- 20% Sudapet

Block 15, RSPOC
- 35% Petronas
- 35% CNPC
- 15% Sudapet
- 10% Express Petroleum & Gas
- 5% Hi Tech

Block 16, Lundin

Block 17, Ansan
- 66% Ansan
- 34% Sudapet

Block A, Sudapak II
- 83% Zafir
- 17% Sudapet

Block B, Total
- 32.5% Total
- 27.5% Kufpec
- 10% Sudapet
- 10% GOSS
- 20% open

Block C, APCO
- 65% Hi Tech
- 17% Sudapet
- 10% Khartoum State
- 8% Heglelg

Block Ea, Free

Endnotes

Explanation of sources:

- Citations for sources available online include a hyperlink to the source.

- Citations that do not include a hyperlink refer to sources accessible through subscription only databases such as Lexis Nexis, or to confidential sources.

- Citations for sources previously quoted feature only an abbreviation of the document title—please refer to the initial citation for full title and location.

[1] World Resources Institute, Economics, Business and the Environment Searchable Database, GDP: GDP per capita, annual growth rate, China, 1970-2005, 2000-2005 (Washington, D.C.: World Resources Institute, 2007), available at http://earthtrends.wri.org/searchable_db/index.php?theme=5.

[2] Energy Information Administration, Official Energy Statistics from the U.S. Government, Searchable Database, *International Country Energy Profiles, China Energy Profile: Ten Year Energy Data Series* (Energy Information Administration, 2007), available at http://tonto.eia.doe.gov/country/country_time_series.cfm?fips=CH.

[3] Joyce Dargay, Dermot Gately, and Martin Sommer, "Vehicle Ownership and Income Growth Worldwide: 1960-2030," *Energy Journal*, Vol. 28, No. 4, January 2007, available at http://www.econ.nyu.edu/dept/courses/gately/DGS_Vehicle%20Ownership_2007.pdf, p. 143.

[4] Ibid., pp. 19, 28.

[5] Energy Information Administration, *China Energy Profile: Data* (2007).

[6] The Brooking Institution, *Statement of Erica S. Downs, China Energy Fellow, Before the U.S.-China Economic and Security Review Commission* (Washington, D.C.: Brookings Institution, August 2006), available at http://www.brookings.edu/~/media/Files/rc/testimonies/2006/0804centralamerica_downs/downs20060804.pdf; Mary Hennock, "China's Global Hunt for Oil," *BBC News*, March 9, 2005 available at http://news.bbc.co.uk/2/hi/business/4191683.stm.

[7] "Rogue Trading," *Foreign Direct Investment Magazine*, June 5, 2006; David Blair, "Oil-Hungry China Takes Sudan Under its Wing," *Telegraph*, April 23, 2005.available at http://www.telegraph.co.uk/news/main.jhtml?xml=/news/2005/04/23/wsud23.xml.

[8] Peter Goodman, "China invests heavily in Sudan's oil industry," *Washington Post*, December 23, 2004, available at http://www.washingtonpost.com/wp-dyn/articles/A21143-2004Dec22.html.

[9] Phillip Liu, "Cross-Strait Scramble for Africa: A Hidden Agenda in China-Africa Cooperation Forum," *Harvard Asia Quarterly*, vol. V, no. 2, Spring 2001, available at http://www.asiaquarterly.com/content/category/8/35/.

[10] Associated Press, "China thanks Africans for defeating Taiwan's bid to join U.N.", Sudan Tribune, September 28, 2007, available at http://www.sudantribune.com/spip.php?page=imprimable&id_article=23973.

[11] Vivienne Walt, "A Khartoum boom, courtesy of China," *Fortune Magazine*, August 6, 2007, available at http://money.cnn.com/2007/08/06/news/international/Sudan_khartoum.fortune/index.htm.

[12] Agence France Presse, "Sudan President Scoffs at Darfur sanctions," *Sudan Tribune*, June 20, 2007, available at http://www.sudantribune.com/spip.php?article22464.

[13] Linda Jakobson, "The Burden of 'non-interference," *China Economic Quarterly*, Quarter 2, 2007, p 14, available at http://www.upi-fiia.fi/doc/0351_ceq2007q2_021foreignpolicy.pdf.

[14] Josh Kurlantzick, "China, Burma, and Sudan: Convincing Argument," *The New Republic Online*, May 11, 2006, available at http://www.carnegieendowment.org/publications/index.cfm?fa=view&id=18329&prog=zch,zgp&proj=zsa; Danna Harman, "China focuses on oil wells, not local needs," *Christian Science Monitor*, June 25, 2007, available at http://www.csmonitor.com/2007/0625/p11s01-woaf.html.

[15] "Rebels tell China 'leave Sudan'," *BBC News*, October 25, 2007, available at http://news.bbc.co.uk/2/hi/africa/7061066.stm.

[16] Associated Press, "74 die in Ethiopian oil field attack," *MSNBC.com*, April 24, 2007, available at http://www.msnbc.msn.com/id/18287943/.

[17] Joseph J. Schatz, "Zambian Hopeful Takes a Swing at China," *Washington Post*, September 25, 2006, available at http://www.washingtonpost.com/wp-dyn/content/article/2006/09/24/AR2006092400915_pf.html.

[18] Reuters, "Sudanese official cautions China on oil investments," *Sudan Tribune*, May 17, 2007, available at http://www.sudantribune.com/spip.php?page=imprimable&id_article=21905.

[19] Kurlantzick, "China, Burma, and Sudan".

[20] European Coalition on Oil in Sudan, *Oil field map*, (Utrecht, The Netherlands, ECOS 2007), available at http://www.ecosonline.org/back/pdf_reports/2007/Oil/oilfieldmap%20Sudan%20ECOS%20aug2007.pdf.

[21] Georgette Gagnon and John Ryle. *Investigation into Oil Development, Conflict and Displacement in Western Upper Nile, Sudan*, Sudan Inter-Agency Reference Group, June 2001, available at http://www.ecosonline.org/back/pdf_reports/2001/SudanReportGagnon103001.pdf

[22] Jeffrey Gettleman, "Far away from Darfur's agony, Khartoum is booming", *International Herald Tribune*, October 24, 2006, available at http://www.iht.com/articles/2006/10/23/africa/web.1024sudan.php.

[23] United Nations Mission in Sudan, *Comprehensive Peace Agreement: Backgrounder*, May 2007, available at http://www.unmis.org/English/cpa.htm.

[24] United Nations Mission in Sudan, *Comprehensive Peace Agreement, Chapter III: Wealth Sharing, article 5.6*, available at http://www.unmis.org/English/documents/cpa-en.pdf, p. 54.

[25] Ibid., Chapter III: Wealth Sharing, article 3.3, p. 52.

[26] Samantha Power, "Dying in Darfur," *The New Yorker*, August 30, 2004, available at http://www.newyorker.com/archive/2004/08/30/040830fa_fact1.

[27] Interview with confidential source within the Government of Southern Sudan.

[28] Central Bank of Sudan, *Annual Report 2000*, (Sudan: Central Bank of Sudan, 2000), Chapt. 8, available at http://www.cbos.gov.sd/english/Periodicals/annual/annual00e/chap8e00.htm.

[29] Central Bank of Sudan, *Annual Report 2006*, (Sudan: Central Bank of Sudan, 2006), Chapt. 8, available at http://www.cbos.gov.sd/english/Periodicals/annual/annual06e/chapter_08.pdf.

[30] Central Bank of Sudan, *Annual Report 2000*, Chapt. 8; Central Bank of Sudan, *Annual Report 2006*, Chapt. 8.

[31] The World Bank Group, *Sudan Data Profile*, (Washington, D.C.: World Bank Group, 2007), available at http://devdata.worldbank.org/external/CPProfile.asp?CCODE=SDN&PTYPE=CP.

[32] Central Bank of Sudan, *Annual Report 2006*, Chapt. 8.

[33] Danna Harman, "China boosts African economies," *Christian Science Monitor*, June 25, 2007, available at http://www.csmonitor.com/2007/0625/p12s01-woaf.html.

[34] Wang Ying, "China's April Oil Imports from Sudan Rise Six Fold," *Bloomberg.com*, May 25, 2007, available at http://www.bloomberg.com/apps/news?pid=20601087&sid=aHLe3XipH8so&refer=hoe; Reuters, "China's Import of Crude Oil from January through June 2007," *Reuters Chinese*, July 22, 2007.

[35] Yet Sudanese exports satisfy only a small portion of China's growing need for oil. In 2006, Sudan was providing approximately seven percent of all Chinese oil imports, making it China's sixth largest supplier of crude oil; the only African country from which China receives more oil is Angola. But China will continue to have to look elsewhere for more oil. The U.S. Department of Energy forecasted that the 2006 increase in China's demand for oil was almost 40 percent of the total increase in world demand for oil. China, which was self-sufficient in oil until 1993, has grown since then to be the third-largest importer of oil worldwide, behind only the United States and Japan. Wang Ying, "China's April Oil Imports from Sudan Rise Six Fold," *Bloomberg.com*; "China chasing gold, iron in Sudan," *Sudan Tribune,* November 6, 2006, available at http://www.bloomberg.com/apps/news?pid=20601087&sid=aHLe3XipH8so&refer=home; "The Increasing Importance of African Oil," *Power and Interest News Report*, March 20, 2006, available at http://www.pinr.com/report.php?ac=view_report&report_id=460&language_id=1; Princeton N. Lyman, "China Ups the Ante in Sudan," *CSIS Africa Policy Forum*, December 1, 2006, available at http://forums.csis.org/africa/?p=17; David Shinn, "Africa, China, the United States, and Oil," *CSIS Africa Policy Forum*, May 2007, available at http://forums.csis.org/africa/?p=34; Vivienne Walt, "A Khartoum boom, courtesy of China," *Fortune Magazine*, August 6, 2007, available at http://money.cnn.com/2007/08/06/news/international/Sudan_khartoum.fortune/index.htm.

[36] Sanusha Naidu, "China and Africa's Natural Resource Sector: A View from South Africa," *CSIS Africa Policy Forum*, April 26, 2007, available at http://forums.csis.org/africa/?p=33.

[37] China National Petroleum Corporation (CNPC), A Leading Global Energy Company, PetroEnergy E&P website, available at http://www.petroenergy-ep.com/cnpc.htm.

[38] "Fortune Global 500, full 2007 list," *Fortune Magazine*, July 23, 2007, available at http://money.cnn.com/magazines/fortune/global500/2007/full_list/index.html.

[39] China National Petroleum Corporation (CNPC), A Leading Global Energy Company, PetroEnergy E&P website, available at http://www.petroenergy-ep.com/cnpc.htm.

[40] "Arms, oil, and Darfur: The evolution of relations between China and Sudan," *Sudan Issue Brief, Small Arms Survey,* July 2007, available at http://wwww.reliefweb.int/rw/rwb.nsf/db900sid/YSAR-765NSX?OpenDocument.

[41] For more information, see Luke Patey, "State Rules, Oil Companies and Armed Conflict in Sudan," Third World Quarterly, Vol. 28, No. 5, 2007 available at http://www.sudantribune.com/spip.php?article22901.

[42] China National Petroleum Corporation (CNPC), A Leading Global Energy Company, PetroEnergy E&P website, Company History, available at http://www.cnpc.com.cn/eng/company/presentation/history/.

[43] Sudan Update, *Sudan Oil and Conflict Timeline*, (Sudan Update), available at http://www.sudanupdate.org/REPORTS/Oil/21oc.html.

[44] European Coalition on Oil in Sudan, *Oil field map*, (Utrecht, The Netherlands, ECOS 2007), available at http://www.ecosonline.org/back/pdf_reports/2007/Oil/oilfieldmap%20Sudan%20ECOS%20aug2007.pdf.

[45] Energy Information Administration, *Sudan Energy Data, Statistics and Analysis: Oil, gas, electricity, coal*, April 2007, available at http://www.eia.doe.gov/cabs/Sudan/Background.html.

[46] Eurasia Group, *China's overseas investments in oil and gas production* (report prepared for the U.S.-China Economic and Security Review Commission) (New York: Eurasia Group, 2006), available at http://www.uscc.gov/researchpapers/2006/oil_gas.pdf, p. 4.

[47] According to an unpublished report circulated among international oil companies in Sudan in 2007, these are at Neem3 and Neem East 5; Khariat 2; Unity 87, 93, 76 and 92; Talih West 12, 8, 9 and 11; and Simbir West 5.

[48] Unpublished report circulated among international oil companies in Sudan.

[49] European Coalition on Oil in Sudan, *Oil field map.*

[50] Petrodar Operating Company website, available at http://www.petrodar.com/profile.html.

[51] Energy Information Administration, *Sudan Energy Data.*

[52] Unpublished report circulated among international oil companies in Sudan.

[53] Energy Information Administration, *Sudan Energy Data.*

[54] Unpublished report circulated among international oil companies in Sudan.

[55] European Coalition on Oil in Sudan, *Oil field map.*

[56] Energy Information Administration, *Sudan Energy Data.*

[57] Unpublished report circulated among international oil companies in Sudan.

[58] China Petroleum Engineering Construction Corporation (CPECC) is now known as China Petroleum Pipeline Engineering Corporation, http://www.cppe.com.cn/English/About_CPPE/Company_Profile.aspx.

[59] Allard K. Lowenstein International Human Rights Clinic and Human Rights Project at Yale Law School, *An Analysis of Select Companies' Operations in Sudan: A Resource for Divestment*, (New Haven, CT: Yale Law School, 2005), p.31-33, available at http://acir.yale.edu/YaleLowensteinSudanReport.pdf.

[60] Ian Johnson, "China Takes Long View in Overseas Oil Projects," *Wall Street Journal* (New York), December 16, 1999.

[61] Human Rights Watch, *Sudan, Oil and Human Rights*, (New York: Human Rights Watch, 2003), available at http://www.hrw.org/reports/2003/sudan1103/26.htm#_ftn1401, FNs 1402, 1404.

[62] "Fortune Global 500 Snapshots: Sinopec," *Fortune Magazine*, July 23, 2007, available at http://money.cnn.com/magazines/fortune/global500/2007/snapshots/10694.html; China Petrochemical Corporation website, available at http://english.sinopecgroup.com/company/.

[63] "Sinopec Group won Contract to Lay Pipeline in Sudan." *Interfax China Business News,* June 21, 2004; Zhongyuan Petroleum Exploration Bureau, *Letter of Congratulations from Sinopec International Engineering Service Corporation (SIPSC),* news release, July 2, 2005, available at http://www.zpebint.com/english/news/listcontentgs.asp?xxid=40701; Zhongyuan Petroleum Exploration Bureau, *ZPEB's Pipeline Section for Package B1 in Block 3/7 in Sudan Fully Completed,* news release, July 2, 2005, available at http://www.zpebint.com/english/news/listcontentgs.asp?xxid=40737; Goodman, "China invests heavily in Sudan's oil industry."

[64] *Interfax,* "Sinopec Group won Contract to Lay Pipeline in Sudan."

[65] Human Rights Watch, *Sudan, Oil and Human Rights*, FN 1401.

[66] European Coalition on Oil in Sudan, *Fact Sheet,* (Utrecht, The Netherlands, ECOS), available at http://www.ecosonline.org/back/pdf_reports/2007/Oil/ECOS%20factsheetII%20October%202007, p. 4.

[67] Greater Nile Petroleum Operating Company website, available at http://www.gnpoc.com/marineTerminal.asp?glink=GL002&plink=PL014.

[68] Petrodar Operating Company website, available at www.petrodar.com.

[69] "Chinese CNPC won tender to build coastal oil terminal in Sudan," *Sudan Tribune*, June 11, 2004, available at http://www.sudantribune.com/spip.php?article3370.

[70] "Asians to Develop Melut," *Africa Energy Intelligence No. 372*, June 23, 2004.

[71] Human Rights Watch, "Sudan, Oil and Human Rights."

[72] Khartoum Refinery Company website, available at http://www.krcsd.com/e-krc/e-index.htm.

[73] Khartoum Refinery Company website.

[74] Goodman, "China invests heavily in Sudan's oil industry."

[75] Eurasia Group, "China's overseas investments in oil and gas production."

[76] Human Rights Watch, "Sudan, Oil and Human Rights", FNs 1005-06.

[77] European Coalition on Oil in Sudan, *Oil Development in Northern Upper Nile, Sudan*, (Utrecht, The Netherlands, ECOS 2007), available at http://www.ecosonline.org/back/pdf_reports/2006/ECOS%20Melut%20Report%202006/ECOS%20Melut%20Report%20final-DEF.pdf.

[78] "China Wins $1.15 billion Sudan railways construction project," *Sudan Tribune*, March 5, 2007, available at http://www.unmis.org/English/2007Docs/mmr-mar05.pdf.

[79] Pieter Tesch and Colin Freeman, "Race to Save First Kingdoms in Africa from Dam Waters," *Telegraph*, September 1, 2006, available at http://www.telegraph.co.uk/news/main.jhtml?xml=/news/2006/01/08/wsudan08.xml&sSheet=/news/2006/01/08/ixworld.html.

[80] Leadership Office of the Hamadab Affected People, International Rivers Network, and The Corner House, *Memorandum on the Merowe Dam Project*, (Berkeley, California: International Rivers Network, 2007), available at http://www.irn.org/programs/merowe/index.php?id=070201memo.html.

[81] Christopher Burke, "Evaluating China's Involvement in Sudan's Merowe Dam Project," *China Monitor*, April 2007, available at http://www.ccs.org.za/downloads/monitors/CCS%20China%20Monitor%20April%2007.pdf.

[82] "Dragon on the Nile: Chinese contractors are well under way on the Merowe dam, one of the biggest projects under construction in the Middle East," *Meed Middle East Economic Digest Weekly Special Report*, May 13, 2005, available for purchase at http://www.alacrastore.com/storecontent/bni/133050766.

[83] Yitzhak Shichor, "Sudan: China's outpost in Africa," *The Jamestown Foundation China Brief*, Vol. V, Issue 21, October 13, 2005, available at http://www.jamestown.org/images/pdf/cb_005_021.pdf.

[84] Hamadab Affected People, International Rivers Network, Corner House, *Memorandum on the Merowe Dam Project*.

[85] Naidu, "China and Africa's Natural Resource Sector"; Hamadab Affected People, International Rivers Network, Corner House, *Memorandum on the Merowe Dam Project*.

[86] "CNPC Subsidiary to Undertake Part of the Transformer Substation Project in Sudan," *Interfax News Agency*, China Energy Report Weekly, August 13, 2004; Meed, "Dragon on the Nile".

[87] Hamadab Affected People, International Rivers Network, Corner House, *Memorandum on the Merowe Dam Project*.

[88] Ibid.

[89] Ibid.

[90] Ibid.

[91] Matthias Muindi, "Dam Could Provoke Water Wars," *News from Africa*, January 2002, available at: http://www.newsfromafrica.org/newsfromafrica/articles/art_609.html; "Chinese companies to finance hydroelectric project in Northern State," *BBC Monitoring Service: Middle East*, September 16, 1997.

[92] Shichor, "Sudan: China's outpost in Africa."

[93] Muindi, "Dam Could Provoke Water Wars."

[94] Associated Press, "4 Jailed Journalists Released in Sudan," *Associated Press*, June 20, 2007.

[95] Lori Pottinger, International Rivers Network. *"Can the Nile States Dam Their Way to Cooperation?: Backgrounder on the Nile Basin Initiative*, (Berkely, California: International Rivers Network, 2004), available at: http://www.irn.org/programs/safrica/pdf/Nile_Briefing.pdf, p.7.

[96] Stephen Kiser, USAF Institute for National Security Studies, Environmental Security Services, *INSS Occasional Paper 35. Water: the Hydraulic Parameter of Conflict in the Middle East and North Africa* (Colorado, 2000: USAF Institute for National Security Studies), available at: http://www.usafa.af.mil/df/inss/OCP/ocp35.pdf, p. 41; "Sudan. Part 9 of 11; Industry and Commerce," *Africa Review World of Information*, April 28, 2006.

[97] International Crisis Group, *Conflict History: Sudan*, (Brussels, Belgium: International Crisis Group, 2006), available at http://www.crisisgroup.org/home/index.cfm?action=conflict_search&l=1&t=1&c_country=101.

[98] International Crisis Group, *A Strategy for Comprehensive Peace in Sudan, Africa Report N. 130*, (Brussels, Belgium: International Crisis Group, July 26, 2007), available at http://www.crisisgroup.org/home/index.cfm?id=4961.

[99] Ibid.

[100] "Four dead in Sudan Kijbar dam protest," *Sudan Tribune*, June 14, 2007, available at http://www.sudantribune.com/spip.php?article22381; Amnesty International, *People's Republic of China: Sustaining conflict and human rights abuses, The flow of arms accelerates*, (London: Amnesty International, 2006), available at http://web.amnesty.org/library/index/engasa170302006.

[101] Associated Press, "4 Jailed Journalists Released in Sudan."

[102] International Crisis Group, *Conflict History: Sudan*.

[103] United Nations Mission in Sudan, "Media Monitoring Report," news release, May 16, 2007, available at: http://www.unmis.org/english/2007Docs/mmr-may16.pdf, p. 9.

[104] Jason Quian and Anne Wu, "China's delicate role on Darfur" *Boston Globe*, July 23, 2007, available at http://www.boston.com/news/world/asia/articles/2007/07/23/chinas_delicate_role_on_darfur/.

[105] Hamadab Affected People, International Rivers Network, Corner House, *Memorandum on the Merowe Dam Project*.

[106] Ibid.

[107] Josh Kurlantzick, Carnegie Endowment for International Peace, *Beijing's Safari: China's move into Africa and its implications for aid, development and governance,* Policy Outlook No. 29, November 2006, available at http://www.carnegieendowment.org/publications/index.cfm?fa=view&id=18833&prog=zch , p. 4.

[108] Harman, "China boosts African economies."

[109] Hamadab Affected People, International Rivers Network, Corner House, "Memorandum on the Merowe Dam Project."

[110] Kurlantzick, "Beijing's Safari", p. 3.

[111] Hamadab Affected People, International Rivers Network, Corner House, "Memorandum on the Merowe Dam Project."

[112] Ibid.

[113] Ibid.

[114] For example, by 1993, the U.S. had listed Sudan as a state sponsor of terrorism. See "Official Pariah Sudan Valuable to America's War on Terrorism, " *LA Times,* April 29, 2005, available at http://www.globalpolicy.org/empire/terrorwar/analysis/2005/0429sudan.htm .

[115] All figures on transfers of small arms, ammunition, parts and accessories taken from the United Nations Commodity Trade Statistics Database (U.N. Comtrade), Commodity Category "Arms and ammunition, parts and accessories thereof (HS1996-93)", available at http://comtrade.un.org/db/default.aspx.

[116] U.N. Comtrade Data is based on customs data reported to the U.N. by governments. In the case of Sudan, most countries, including China, don't fully report their exports to Sudan. It is therefore possible that Sudan's reported figures are lower than the true value of arms imports.

[117] China's transfers of major conventional weapons are also difficult to evaluate as China did not submit data to the U.N. Register of Conventional Arms in from 1998 to 2006. In August 2007, China submitted a report for 2006 which does not include any transfers to Sudan. See U.N. Register of Conventional Arms, Reporting country: China, Calendar year: 2006, Date of Submission: 31 August 2007, available at http://disarmament.un.org/UN_REGISTER.nsf; "China withdraws from register in protest", *Jane's Defence Weekly,* 18 November 1998; Amnesty International, "People's Republic of China Sustaining conflict and human rights abuses" ; Ministry of Foreign Affairs of the People's Republic of China, *U.N. Register of Conventional Arms,* May 21, 2007, http://www.mfa.gov.cn/eng/wjb/zzjg/jks/kjlc/cgjkwt/cgjm/t321038.htm .

[118] Shichor, "Sudan: China's Outpost in Africa."

[119] Stockholm International Peace Research Institute, online database, *Arms Trade Register*; Stockholm International Peace Research Institute, online database, *Trend Indicator Value Table: Sudan, 1960-2006,* (Stockholm: Stockholm International Peace Research Institute, 2006), available at http://armstrade.sipri.org/arms_trade/values.php .

[120] SIPRI, Arms Trade Register, Trend Indicator Value Table: Sudan, 1960-2006

[121] Stockholm International Peace Research Institute, online database, *Military Expenditures: Sudan,* (Stockholm: Stockholm International Peace Research Institute, 2006), available at http://first.sipri.org/non_first/milex.php .

[122] SIPRI, Arms Trade Register, Trend Indicator Value Table: Sudan, 1960-2006.

[123] Stockholm International Peace Research Institute, online database, *Transfers of major conventional weapons: sorted by supplier. Deals with deliveries or orders made for year range 1997 to 2006,* information generated: 11 June 2007, available at www.sipri.org/contents/armstrad/REG_EXP_CHI_97-06.pdf/download.

[124] United Nations Panel of Experts on Sudan, *Final Report from the Panel of Experts,* (New York: United Nations, 2006), S/2006/65, available at http://www.un.org/sc/committees/1591/reports.shtml, p.37.

[125] "Murder Made in China," *International Herald Tribune,* July 4, 2006, available at http://www.iht.com/articles/2006/07/04/opinion/edchina.php.

[126] SIPRI, 'Transfers of major conventional weapons: sorted by supplier"; Human Rights Watch, "Darfur: Indiscriminate Bombing Warrants U.N. Sanctions," Sept. 6, 2006, at http://hrw.org/english/docs/2006/09/06/sudan14138.htm.

[127] Andrei Chang, United Press International, "Analysis: China Sells Arms to Sudan," *United Press International,* Feb. 15, 2008, available at http://www.upi.com/International_Security/Industry/Analysis/2008/02/15/analysis_china_sells_arms_to_sudan/7530/.

[128] Ibid.

[129] Ibid.

[130] United Nations Security Council, *Resolution 1556,* (New York: United Nations, 2004), S/RES/1556; United Nations Security Council, *Resolution 1591,* (New York: United Nations, 2004), S/RES/1591.

[131] Daniel Byman & Roger Cliff, RAND Corporation, *"China's Arms Sales: Motivations and Implications,* (Santa Monica, CA: RAND Corporation, 1999), available at http://www.rand.org/pubs/monograph_reports/MR1119 .

[132] Esther Pan, Council on Foreign Relations, *"China, Africa, and Oil"*, January 26, 2007, available at http://www.cfr.org/publication/9557/.

[133] United Nations Security Council, *Resolution 1556.*

[134] United Nations Security Council, *Resolution 1591.*

[135] Since 1994, the European Union has also upheld an arms embargo on all transfers of arms, munitions, and military equipment to Sudan, see Council of the European Union, Council common position concerning an arms embargo on Sudan, (Brussels, Belgium: European Union, 1994), 94/165/CFSP, available at http://www.sipri.org/contents/expcon/eu_sudan01.html ;Council of the European Union, Council common position concerning the imposition of an embargo on arms, munitions, and military equipment on Sudan, (Brussels, Belgium: European Union, 2004) 2004/31/CFSP, available at http://www.legaltext.ee/text/en/PH2839.htm.

[136] Amnesty International, "People's Republic of China: Sustaining conflict and human rights abuses"; Daniel Pepper, "War follows refugees to Darfur: From inside Sudan, Chadian rebels launch attacks on their home," *San Francisco Chronicle,* March 13, 2006; Human Rights Watch, "Sudan, Oil and Human Rights"; United Nations Panel of Experts on Sudan, *Final Reports from the Panel of Experts,* (New York: United Nations, 2006), S/2006/65 (January 2006), S/2006/250 (April 2006), and S/2006/795 (October 2006), available at http://www.un.org/sc/committees/1591/reports.shtml.

[137] In an interview dated May 8, 2007 "Chinese Foreign Ministry spokeswoman Jiang Yu dismissed suggestions that China was continuing to sell arms to Sudan, saying Beijing ha[d] strict rules about its arms exports". She said such accusations were 'totally unreasonable.'" Reuters, "China, Russia breach Darfur arms embargo—Amnesty," *Reuters*, May 8, 2007, available at http://www.alertnet.org/thenews/newsdesk/L08646701.htm.

[138] Opheera McDoom, Reuters, "China Urges Dialogue Not Sanctions on Darfur," *Reuters*, Sept. 2, 2007, available at http://www.reuters.com/article/africaCrisis/idUSMCD230720.

[139] "China's arms sales to Sudan are limited: Envoy," *People's Daily Online,* July 6, 2007, available at http://english.peopledaily.com.cn/90001/90776/6209559.html.

[140] "China not supplying arms for violence-wracked Darfur," *Sudan Tribune,* May 9, 2007, available at http://www.sudantribune.com/spip.php?article21778 .

[141] United Nations Panel of Experts on Sudan, "Final Report from the Panel of Experts", October 2006.

[142] People's Republic of China, State Council of the People's Republic of China and the Central Military Commission of the People's Republic of China, *Regulations of the People's Republic of China on Administration of Arms Export,* Promulgated by Decree No. 366, August 15, 2002, effective November 15, 2002, available at http://www.gov.cn/english/laws/2005-07/25/content_16975.htm.

[143] Chinese arms export are ruled by the "Regulations of the People's Republic of China onAdministration of Arms Export", the latest version of which was promulgated on August 15, 2002 by Decree No. 366 of the State Council of the People's Republic of China and the Central Military Commission of the People's Republic of China, and entered into force on 15 November 2002. Article 5 of those regulations reads as follows: "Article 5.The following principles shall be observed in exporting arms: (1) conduciveness to the capability for just self-defence of the recipient country; (2) no injury to the peace, security and stability of the region concerned and the world as a whole; (3) no interference in the internal affairs of the recipient country. Available at hhttp://www.gov.cn/english/laws/200507/25/content_16975.htm

[144] Sudan Issue Brief, "Arms, oil, and Darfur", p. 6.

[145] Ibid., FN 34.

[146] "Chinese, Sudanese senior military leaders hold talks on closer ties," *Xinhua News Agency*, Apr. 4, 2007, available at http://www.sudantribune.com/spip.php?article21164.

[147] Danna Harman, "How China's support of Sudan shields a regime called 'genocidal," *Christian Science Monitor,* June 26, 2007, available at http://www.csmonitor.com/2007/0626/p01s08-woaf.htm.

[148] Agence France Presse, "Sudan president scoffs at Darfur sanctions."

[149] Gagnon and Ryle. "Oil Development, Conflict and Displacement in Western Upper Nile".

[150] Koang Tut Doh and Kur Yai Nop, South Sudanese Friends International, Inc., *Looming Disaster in Western Upper Nile Region: A Political Eye Witness Report from the Field*, (Nairobi, Kenya: South Sudanese Friends International, 2000), available at http://southsudanfriends.org/ORCD/WUNPoliticalReport.html.

[151] Executive Order 13400, *Blocking Property of Persons in Connection with the Conflict in Sudan's Darfur Region*, April 26, 2006, available at http://www.presidency.ucsb.edu/ws/print.php?pid=72507.

[152] Christian Aid, *The Scorched Earth: Oil and War in Sudan*, (New York: Christian Aid, 2001), available at http://212.2.6.41/indepth//0103suda/sudanoi2.htm.

[153] United Nations Panel of Experts on Sudan, *Final Report from the Panel of Experts*, (New York: United Nations, 2006), S/2006/65, available at http://www.un.org/sc/committees/1591/reports.shtml, p.37.

[154] Chandra Leika Sriram, "China, Human rights and the Sudan," *Jurist Legal News and Research*, January 30, 2007, available at http://jurist.law.pitt.edu/forumy/2007/01/china-human-rights-and-Sudan.php.

[155] Coalition for International Justice, *Soil and Oil: Dirty Business in Sudan*, (Washington, D.C., Coalition for International Justice, 2006), available at http://www.ecosonline.org/back/pdf_reports/2006/reports/Soil_and_Oil_Dirty_Business_in_Sudan.pdf , p. 23.

[156] Byman and Cliff, "China's Arms Sales: Motivations and Implications".

[157] Pan, "China, Africa, and Oil."

[158] Richard F. Grimmet, Congressional Research Service, *Conventional Arms Transfers to Developing Nations, 1998-2005*, (Washington, D.C.: Congressional Research Service, 2006), available at http://www.fas.org/sgp/crs/weapons/RL33696.pdf, p. 62.

[159] From 1998 to 2005, China's share of annual international arms deliveries was just over 2.4 percent of worldwide totals. This figure is slightly more than six percent of those of the world's largest arms exporter, the United States. See Richard F. Grimmet, Congressional Research Service, *Conventional Arms Transfers to Developing Nations, 1998-2005*, (Washington, D.C.: Congressional Research Service, 2006), available at http://www.fas.org/sgp/crs/weapons/RL33696.pdf, p. 85; Congressional Research Service Reports for 1993-2000, 1994-2001, 1995-2002, 1996-2003, 1997-2004, 1998-2005; Federation of American Scientists, *U.S. Arms Transfers: Government Data, Table 2C Regional Arms Deliveries by Supplier*, (Washington, D.C.: Federation of American Scientists), available at http://www.fas.org/asmp/profiles/worldfms.html.

[160] Russia is estimated to have provided almost three-quarters of imports for Sudan's current military arsenal. See Shichor, "Sudan: China's outpost in Africa"; SIPRI, *Arms Trade Register*.

[161] Human Rights Watch, "Sudan, Oil and Human Rights."

[162] Goodman, "China invests heavily in Sudan's oil industry."

[163] Interviews with confidential source within the Government of Southern Sudan, 2007.

[164] Reuters, "China tells Sudan to ensure safety after attack claim," *Sudan Tribune*, October 26, 2007, available at http://www.sudantribune.com/spip.php?article24434.

[165] "Militarization of Sudan: A preliminary review of arms flows and holdings," *Sudan Issue Brief, Small Arms Survey*, April 2007, available at http://www.smallarmssurvey.org/files/portal/spotlight/sudan/Sudan_pdf/SIB%206%20militarization.pdf , p. 9.

[166] John Young, "Emerging North South Tensions and Prospects for a return to War," *Sudan Issue Brief, Small Arms Survey*, July 2007, available at http://www.smallarmssurvey.org/files/portal/spotlight/sudan/Sudan_pdf/SWP%207%20North-South%20tensions.pdf.

[167] Skye Wheeler, "SAF still in the South," *Gurtong Peace Trust*, October 7, 2007, available at http://www.gurtong.org/ResourceCenter/weeklyupdates/wu_contents.asp?wkupdt_id=893 &vswuOrder=Sorter_YWCode&vswuDir=ASC&vswuPage=2.

[168] Mikhail Zygar, Global Research "Behind the U.N. Security Council Resolution: Chinese, Russian and Indian Oil interests in the Sudan," news release, September 19, 2004, available at http://www.globalresearch.ca/index.php?context=va&aid=612.

[169] "Chinese U.N. Envoy says Sudan Sanctions 'Complicate' Situation," *Xinhua News Agency*, July 30, 2004.

[170] United Nations Security Council, Explanatory Remarks by Chinese Permanent Representative Mr. Wang Guangya at Security Council on Sudan Darfur Draft Resolution, (New York: United Nations Security Council, September 18, 2004) available at http://www.fmprc.gov.cn/ce/ceun/eng/xw/t158034.htm.

[171] "Sudan: Khartoum Relieved As U.N. Resolution Falls Short," *All Africa News*, September 21, 2004.

[172] Maggie Farley, "Security Council Votes to Provide Aid after End to Sudan Civil War," *LA Times*, November 20, 2004, available at http://www.publicinternationallaw.org/docs/PNW4/PNW.22Nov_04.html#Sudan.

[173] Ibid.

[174] Evelyn Leopold, Reuters, "Annan Calls Emergency Sudan Session of U.N. Council," *Reuters,* March 7, 2005, available at http://www.globalpolicy.org/security/issues/sudan/2005/0307closedmeet.htm. Evelyn Leopold, Reuters, "U.N. Council Votes for Sanctions on Darfur Offenders," *Reuters*, March 30, 2005, available at http://www.globalpolicy.org/security/issues/sudan/2005/0330sanctionspass.htm.

[175] Reuters, "U.N. delays Sudan sanctions by three months," *Sudan Tribune*, July 7, 2005, available at http://www.sudantribune.com/spip.php?article10526.

[176] "Sudanese government expresses sorrow over U.N. resolution 1591," *China View News*, March 30, 2005, available at http://www1.china.org.cn/english/international/124326.htm.

[177] Christine Chaumeau, "Beijing's calculated prudence," *International Justice Tribune*, October 23, 2006.

[178] There were twenty Resolutions in total related to Darfur, but fourteen of those addressed substantive issues. United Nations Security Council, *Resolution 1769*, (New York: United Nations Security Council, July 31, 2007), S/RES/1769; United Nations Security Council, *Resolution 1755*, (April 30, 2007), S/RES/1755; United Nations Security Council, *Resolution 1714* (October 6, 2006), S/RES/1714; United Nations Security Council, *Resolution 1713* (September 29, 2006), S/RES/1714; United Nations Security Council, *Resolution 1709*, (September 22, 2006), S/RES/1709; United Nations Security Council, *Resolution 1706*, (August 31, 2006) S/RES/1706; United Nations Security Council, *Resolution 1679*, (May 16, 2006), S/RES/1679; United Nations Security Council, *Resolution 1672*, (April 25, 2006), S/RES/1672; United Nations Security Council, *Resolution 1665*, (March 29, 2006) S/RES/1665; United Nations Security Council, *Resolution 1663*, (March 24, 2006) S/RES/1663); United Nations Security Council, *Resolution 1651*, (December 21, 2005) S/RES/1651; United Nations Security Council, *Resolution 1593*, (March 31, 2005), S/RES/1593; United Nations Security Council, *Resolution 1591*, (March 29, 2005), S/RES/1591; United Nations Security Council, *Resolution 1590*, (March 24, 2005), S/RES/1590; United Nations Security Council, *Resolution 1588*, (March 17, 2005) S/RES/1588; United Nations Security Council, *Resolution 1585*, (March 10, 2005), S/RES/1585; United Nations Security Council, *Resolution 1574*, (November 19, 2004), S/RES/1574; United Nations Security Council, *Resolution 1564*, (September 18, 2004), S/RES/1564; United Nations Security Council, *Resolution 1556*, (July 30, 2004), S/RES/1556; United Nations Security Council, *Resolution 1547*, (June 11, 2004), S/RES/1547.

[179] China weakened text in Resolutions 1556, 1564, 1574, 1591, 1593, 1672, 1679, 1706, and 1769 and abstained on Resolutions 1556, 1564, 1591, 1593, and 1706.

[180] Reuters, "China played determinant role for Darfur force acceptance—envoy," Sudan Tribune, September 12, 2007, available at http://www.sudantribune.com/spip.php?page=imprimable&id_article=23708.

[181] United Nations, "Third Committee Approves Eight Draft Resolutions on Human Rights, Right to Development, Globalization, Iran, Sudan," news release, November 30, 2001, available at http://www.un.org/News/Press/docs/2001/gashc3677.doc.htm; "Darfur issue can only be solved through political means: Chinese official," *China View News*, April 21, 2005.

[182] United Nations, "Human Rights Council Discusses Reports on Situation of Human Rights in Sudan and Belarus," news release, September 27, 2006, available at http://www.unog.ch/unog/website/news_media.nsf/(httpNewsByYear_en)/585236C1A3977DFCC12571F6004FF0AE.

[183] Ibid.

[184] United nations, "Human Rights Council Notes with Concern Serious Human Rights and Humanitarian Situation in Darfur," news release, November 28, 2006, available at http://www.unog.ch/unog/website/news_media.nsf/(httpNewsByYear_en)/62C6B3F928618CCEC12572340046C4BB.

[185] United Nations, *Human Rights Council 4th Special Session on the Human Rights Situation in Darfur, Explanations after the vote*, (Geneva: United Nations), available with password at http://portal.ohchr.org/portal/page/portal/HRCExtranet/4SpecialSession/DraftDecision/China.pdf.

[186] International Service for Human Rights, "Daily Update," March 16, 2007, available at http://www.ishr.ch/hrm/council/dailyupdates/session_004/16_march_2007.pdf.

[187] Wasil Ali, "ICC Prosecutor is a junior employee doing cheap work," *Sudan Tribune*, June 11, 2007, available at http://www.sudantribune.com/spip.php?article22313.

[188] "Special train carrying Chinese aid leaves for Darfur," *People's Daily Online*, September 25, 2007, available at http://english.peopledaily.com.cn/90001/90777/6270218.html.

[189] Reuters, "China played determinant role for Darfur force acceptance—envoy."

[190] "African Union extends its peacekeeping mission in Darfur, says it will handover to U.N. when peace agreement reached," *Associated Press*, March 10, 2006; African Union discusses whether to hand over Darfur peacekeeping to U.N., *Associated Press*, March 10, 2006.

[191] African Union Peace and Security Council, *Communique of the 46th Meeting*, (Addis Ababa, Ethiopia, African Union, March 10, 2006), available at http://www.issafrica.org/AF/RegOrg/unity_to_union/pdfs/centorg/PSC/2006/46com.pdf.

[192] United Nations Security Council, "Security Council Endorses African Union Decision on Need for Concrete Steps in Transition to United Nations Operation in Darfur," news release, May16, 2006, available at http://www.un.org/News/Press/docs/2006/sc8721.doc.htm.

[193] "U.N. Aims to Hasten Dispatch of Troops to Darfur," *LA Times,* May 17, 2006.

[194] United Nations Security Council, *Meeting Record of 5519th meeting*, (New York: United Nations Security Council, August 31, 2006), S/PV.5519, available at http://daccessdds.un.org/doc/UNDOC/PRO/N06/484/22/PDF/N0648422.pdf?OpenElement.

[195] Reuters, "Sudan says U.N. force would create second Iraq," *Reuters*, November 3, 2006, available at http://www.alertnet.org/thenews/newsdesk/PEK293358.htm.

[196] Robert F. Worth, "Sudan Says It Will Accept U.N.-African Peace Force in Darfur," *New York Times*, November 16, 2006, available at http://www.nytimes.com/2006/11/17/world/africa/17darfur.html.

[197] Chris Buckley, Reuters "China Claims Credit on Darfur, Raises Arms Concern," *Reuters*, July 5, 2007, available at http://uk.reuters.com/article/worldNews/idUKPEK3477120070705.

[198] Daniel Schearf, "China takes credit for Sudan allowing peacekeepers," *Voice of America*, July 5, 2007, available at http://www.voanews.com/tibetan/archive/2007-07/2007-07-05-voa4.cfm.

[199] Wasil Ali, "China voices opposition to sanctions on Sudan," *Sudan Tribune*, March 19, 2007, available at http://www.sudantribune.com/spip.php?article20853.

[200] Alfred De Montesquieu, Associated Press, "China's Hu Presses Sudan for Progress on Darfur," *Washington Post*, February 3, 2007, available at http://www.washingtonpost.com/wp-dyn/content/article/2007/02/02/AR2007020201753.html.

[201] "China calls for change on Darfur," *BBC News*, April 9, 2007, available at http://news.bbc.co.uk/2/hi/africa/6538401.stm.

[202] "Sanctions not helpful for resolving Darfur issues," *China View News*, May 29, 2007, available at http://news.xinhuanet.com/english/2007-05/29/content_6170801.htm.

[203] Ibid.

[204] Reuters, "China Aims for Constructive Darfur Role," *The Age*, May 24, 2007, available at http://www.theage.com.au/news/WORLD/China-aims-for-constructive-Darfur-role/2007/05/24/1179601574257.html.

[205] Wasil Ali, "China uses economic leverage to pressure Sudan on Darfur," *Sudan Tribune*, March 6, 2007, available at http://www.sudantribune.com/spip.php?article20615; Lee Feinstein, "China and Sudan," *TPM Café*, April 24, 2007, available at http://www.tpmcafe.com/blog/americaabroad/2007/apr/24/china_and_sudan.

[206] John D. Negroponte and Jendayi Frazer, *Briefing on Their Recent Travel to Africa, transcript* (Washington, D.C., U.S. Department of State, April 23, 2007), available at http://www.state.gov/s/d/2007/83417.htm.

[207] Joint NGO report, including Human Rights First, *UNAMID Deployment on the Brink,* (New York: December 2007), available at http://www.humanrightsfirst.info/pdf/071221-ij-UNAMID-joint-report.pdf

[208] U.N. News, "Sudanese army elements attack UN convoy; Ban Ki-moon protests", *U.N. News*, January 8, 2008, available at http://www.un.org/apps/news/story.asp?NewsID=25231&Cr=Darfur&Cr1

[209] Human Rights First, "China Shield's Sudan in the Security Council After ICC Prosecutor's Report", December 17, 2007, available at http://www.humanrightsfirst.org/media/darfur/2007/alert/396/index.htm

[210] Sebastian Mallaby, "A Palace for Sudan: China's No-Strings Aid Undermines the West," *Washington Post*, February 5, 2007, available at http://www.washingtonpost.com/wp-dyn/content/article/2007/02/04/AR2007020401047.html.

[211] Interview with confidential source within the Government of Southern Sudan, 2007.

[212] Confidential interview with oil and gas executive in Southern Sudan, 2007.

213 Interview with confidential source within SPLM, 2007.

214 Interview with confidential source within SPLM, 2007.

215 Confidential interview with former official of foreign government in Southern Sudan, 2007.

216 Confidential interview with former official of foreign government in Southern Sudan, 2007.

217 Interview with confidential source within the Government of Southern Sudan, 2007.

218 "Minister of Foreign Affairs on First Vice President visit to China," *Suna News Agency*, July 16, 2007.

219 Confidential interview with oil & gas executive in Southern Sudan, 2007; discussions with confidential sources within SPLM, 2007.

220 Confidential interviews with officials of major international donor bodies active in South Sudan, 2007.

221 Confidential interviews with a former official of a foreign government in South Sudan; with a western diplomat; and with an engineer with a Chinese contractor, 2007.

222 "China to Finance Development Projects in South Sudan," *Sudan Tribune*, September 1, 2007, available at http://www.sudantribune.com/spip.php?article23541.

223 This table is derived from information noted elsewhere in this report. It is not intended to be comprehensive but rather to give an overall view of the issue.

224 Africa Energy Intelligence, "Asians to Develop Melut."

225 Ibid.

226 Lee Feinstein, China and Sudan

227 Middle East Business Digest. "Sudan Gets $3.0 Mln Chinese Loan To Support Technical Education". July 9, 2004. Available at: http://www.lexis.com/research/retrieve/frames?_m=4e853a456f3631f6de60ec4bb911403e&csvc=bl&cform=bool&_fmtstr=CITE&docnum=1&_startdoc=1&wchp=dGLzVlz-zSkAz&_md5=7fdc70f40dc7dc250e804620ce93732f

228 U.S. says Darfur violence is genocide, United Press International, September 9, 2004

229 Security Council Votes to Provide Aid After End to Sudan Civil War, Maggie Farley, *LA Times*, 11/20/2004 http://www.publicinternationallaw.org/docs/PNW4/PNW.22Nov_04.html#Sudan

230 Reuters, March 7, 2005, Annan Calls Emergency Sudan Session of U.N. Council, http://www.globalpolicy.org/security/issues/sudan/2005/0307closedmeet.htm . Reuters, U.N. Council Votes for Sanctions on Darfur Offenders (March 30, 2005), http://www.globalpolicy.org/security/issues/sudan/2005/0330sanctionspass.htm

231 Sudanese government expresses sorrow over U.N. resolution 1591 Xinhua General News Service March 30, 2005

232 Mr. Wang Guangya, explanation of the Chinese vote, Security Council, 5158th meeting, Thursday, 31 March 2005,

233 U.N. delays Sudan sanctions by three months, Reuters, July 7, 2005 http://www.sudantribune.com/spip.php?article10526

234 China Daily. "China builds Sudan's largest power project". April 12, 2005. Available at: Factiva.

235 CNPC Annual Report 2006, Overseas Oil & Gas Operations, http://www.cnpc.com.cn/Resource/eng/img/AnnualReport/Overseas_Oil_and_Gas_Operations.pdf

236 The Sudan Tribune. "$6 million for Education Programs in Southern Sudan". August 22, 2005. Available at: http://www.sudantribune.com/spip.php?article11190

237 Lee Feinstein, China and Sudan

238 Security Council Endorses African Union Decision On Need For Concrete, Steps In Transition To United Nations Operation In Darfur, U.N. Department of Public Information, 16 May 2006

239 The World; U.N. Aims to Hasten Dispatch of Troops to Darfur; Peacekeepers would take control of AU forces. Security Council also threatens sanctions for anyone who violates the recent peace accord. Los Angeles Times May 17, 2006

240 United States Still Pursuing Peace in Darfur, State's Bolton Says Africa News July 27, 2006

241 Security Council, 5519th meeting, Thursday, 31 August 2006

242 Sudan Says It Will Accept U.N.-African Peace Force in Darfur, New York Times, November 16, 2006 http://www.nytimes.com/2006/11/17/world/africa/17darfur.html

[243] Sudan says U.N. Darfur force would create second Iraq, Reuters, November 3, 2006 http://www.alertnet.org/thenews/newsdesk/PEK293358.htm

[244] Sudan Tribune. "Chinese Oil CNPC to Improve Sudan Social Facilities". Jan.31, 2007. Available at: http://www.sudantribune.com/spip.php?article20044

[245] http://www.washingtonpost.com/wp-dyn/content/article/2007/02/02/AR2007020201753.html

[246] Economist Intelligence Unit - Business Africa. "Travel & tourism: Sudan". April 1, 2007. Issue no. 304. Available at: http://global.factiva.com/ha/default.aspx

[247] National Union of Rail, Maritime, and Transport Workers website. Taken from Sudan Tribune article, March 5, 2007. "China Wins $1.15 billion Sudan railways construction project".

[248] Chan, John. Asian Tribune. "Hu rejects accusations that China has colonial ambitions in Africa." Feb. 16, 2007. Available at: http://www.asiantribune.com/index.php?q=node/4562

[249] http://news.xinhuanet.com/english/2007-05/29/content_6170801.htm

[250] Sudan, China Sign Air Freight Agreement, May 15, 2007, Sudan Vision Daily http://www.smc.sd/en/artopic.asp?artID=14577&aCK=EA

[251] "CNPC signs new Sudan oil block contract, may revive pressure to divest in listed arm," *Interfax China*, July 8, 2007. http://www.interfax.cn/displayarticle.asp?aid=25495&slug=CHINA-ENERGY-OIL

[252] Sudan Issue Brief, "Arms, oil, and Darfur".

[253] Human Rights Watch, *Sudan: In the Name of God*, (New York: Human Rights Watch, 1994), available at http://www.hrw.org/reports/1994/sudan/; United Nations General Assembly, *Situation of Human Rights in Sudan*, (New York: United Nations, 1993), A/RES/48/147, available at http://www.un.org/documents/ga/res/48/a48r147.htm.

[254] U.S. Department of State, *State Sponsors of Terrorism*, (Washington, D.C.: U.S. Department of State), available at http://www.state.gov/s/ct/c14151.htm .

[255] Human Rights Watch, "Sudan, Oil and Human Rights."

[256] Ibid., pp. 105 and 135.

[257] Ibid, p. 124 138; Danish Institute for International Studies, *A Complex Reality: The Strategic Behavior of Multinational Oil Corporations and the New Wars in Sudan*, (Copenhagen, Denmark, Danish Institute for International Studies, 2006), available at http://www.diis.dk/sw21249.asp.

[258] Danish Institute for International Studies, "A Complex Reality".

[259] Scott Anderson, "How did Darfur Happen?" *New York Times Magazine*, October 17, 2004, available at http://www.nytimes.com/2004/10/17/magazine/17DARFUR.html .

[260] Coalition for International Justice, "Soil and Oil".

[261] Human Rights Watch, "Sudan, Oil and Human Rights", Appendix C.

[262] "Executive Order 13067 of November 3, 1997: Blocking Sudanese Government Property and Prohibiting Transactions with Sudan," 62 FR 59989, November 5, 1997, available at http://www.treas.gov/offices/enforcement/ofac/legal/eo/13067.pdf.

[263] United Nations Security Council, *Resolution 1372*, (New York: United Nations Security Council, 2001), S/RES/1372, available at http://www.un.org/Docs/scres/2001/sc2001.htm.

[264] Power, "Dying in Darfur"; Gettleman, "War in Sudan?"

[265] Anderson, "How did Darfur Happen?"

[266] Ibid.

[267] Ibid.

[268] International Commission of Inquiry on Darfur, Report of the International Commission of Inquiry on Darfur to the United Nations Secretary-General: Pursuant to Security Council Resolution 1564 *of 18 September 2004* (New York: United Nations, 2005), available at http://www.un.org/News/dh/sudan/com_inq_darfur.pdf, para. 57.

[269] Power, "Dying in Darfur."

[270] International Crisis Group, "Conflict History: Sudan."

[271] International Commission of Inquiry on Darfur, "Report of the International Commission of Inquiry", para. 68; Anderson, "How did Darfur Happen?"

[272] Anderson, "How did Darfur Happen?"

[273] *In the Case of The Prosecutor v. Ahmad Muhammad Harun and Ali Muhammad al Abd-Al-Rahman*, ICC-02/05-01/07, April 27, 2007, available at http://www.icc-cpi.int/library/cases/ICC-02-05-01-07-1_English.pdf, para. 65.

[274] United Nations High Commissioner for Human Rights, *Fifth periodic report of the United Nations High Commissioner for Human Rights on the situation of human rights in the Sudan*, (Geneva: United Nations, October 2006), available at http://www.ohchr.org/Documents/Countries/5thOHCHRsept06.pdf, para. 26.

[275] Interviews with confidential former official of foreign intelligence service in Sudan, 2007.

[276] "Darfur peace talks stall as rebels boycott meeting," *The Guardian*, October 29, 2007, available at http://www.guardian.co.uk/sudan/story/0,,2201227,00.html.

1787888

Made in the USA